UX Design 2020

The ultimate beginner's guide to user experience

Theo Farrington

Copyright © 2020 by Theo Farrington
All rights reserved.
ISBN-13: 9798657731040

This document is geared towards providing exact and reliable information with regards to the topic and issue covered. The publication is sold with the idea that the publisher is not required to render accounting, officially permitted, or otherwise, qualified services. If advice is necessary, legal or professional, a practiced individual in the profession should be ordered.

- From a Declaration of Principles which was accepted and approved equally by a Committee of the American Bar Association and a Committee of Publishers and Associations.

In no way is it legal to reproduce, duplicate, or transmit any part of this document in either electronic means or in printed format. Recording of this publication is strictly prohibited and any storage of this document is not allowed unless with written permission from the publisher. All rights reserved.

The information provided herein is stated to be truthful and consistent, in that any liability, in terms of inattention or otherwise, by any usage or abuse of any policies, processes, or directions contained within is the solitary and utter responsibility of the recipient reader. Under no circumstances will any legal responsibility or blame be held against the publisher for any reparation, damages, or monetary loss due to the information herein, either directly or indirectly.

Respective authors own all copyrights not held by the publisher.

The information herein is offered for informational purposes solely, and is universal as so. The presentation of the information is without contract or any type of guarantee assurance.
The trademarks that are used are without any consent, and the publication of the trademark is without permission or backing by the trademark owner. All trademarks and brands within this book are for clarifying purposes only and are the owned by the owners themselves, not affiliated with this document.

Table of Contents

Foreword
12

What is UX?
17

What is Design
18

UX is for User Experience
20

UX is for the People
22

UX is Everywhere
25

A brief History of UX
33

What is UX for?
38

UX for Interfaces
38

UX for Products
39

UX for Content
40

UX for Services
41

UX for Spaces
43

The Principles

Design Thinking — 45

The 7 Golden Rules of UX Design — 45

1. Clarity — 47
2. Intuition — 47
3. Digestibility — 48
4. Flow — 49
5. Familiarity — 49
6. Delight — 50
7. Feedback — 51

Your perspective VS User Perspective — 52

Design for Real Life — 54

Focus on the Solutions — 56

Key Concepts to Keep in Mind — 58

The Design Process

— 60

1. Goal Definition and Problem Setting — 64

— 66

2. User Research

74

The Research Learning Spiral

82

User Groups

95

User Interviews

98

Online Surveys

105

Card Sorting

111

Personas

117

3. Design and Develop

125

Wireframing

127

Information Architecture

133

User Journey

144

User Flows

147

Prototyping

152

4. Test and Measure

161

Usability testing

162

A/B test

169

Biometrics

172

Data and analytics

175

Reports

178

5. Launch and Iterate

181

Visual Design Principles

184

Gestalt basics

186

Visual Design Toolkit

197

Visual Weight

197

Room to breathe

199

Using motion to convey meaning

201

Going Further

205

Human behavior and motivations

205

Create Trust

212

The Empathy Map

217

Accessibility

219

Customized experiences

223

The Essential Value of UX Design
228

User Benefits
229

Product Benefits
231

Business Benefits
234

UX Design Jobs
239

What does a UX designer do?
239

The disciplines of UX Design
240

Common tools
246

Conclusion
253

Get in touch
261

About the Author
262

Foreword

It's not just how it looks like and feels like. Design it's how it works.

– Steve Jobs

Let's clear the way right off the bat. UX is not UI. User Experience and User Interface inevitably crop up when talking about UX, but it is important to acknowledge the differences because, indeed, UX and UI are two different things.

User interface design is about the look and functioning of a product. The term is rather eloquent itself. It is about interfaces. The surface with which a user interacts, the visual design of screens, lockscreens, menus, buttons, scrollbars, and so on. Everything a user interacts with during the navigation inside a mobile app or website. UI designers cover everything from color palettes, to animations and typography.

Instead, user experience design is about the user's journey to solve a problem. It is about the usability of a mobile app or a product. It focuses on the navigational touchpoints of a mobile app, the flow, and how easy it is for the user to navigate to the desired goal. UX Design is about the whole experience.

UX and UI intersect and are essential to one another. The product interface has a huge impact on the overall experience, but it is useless if the overall experience is not well researched and designed by the UX design.

But if a beautiful interface design is easily recognizable, how can one recognize a beautifully designed experience?

Well, a good user experience is simple. As simple as breathing. Human beings breathe an average of 23.000 times a day. Have you ever noticed it? Unless you practice meditation, it is unlikely you have. Good design is the same, the best experience is no experience. So, the first answer to our question is: if you don't perceive the design, then it's good design.

But this is only half of the answer. A good experience is invisible and makes a difference. Breathing makes a huge difference, right? This is what a great UX Design does.

Product, apps, services should be so simple that even in an emergency, a beginner should be able to understand it within ten seconds. The user should be able to understand the meaning and rules of its elements almost immediately, guided by the invisible hand of the UX designer, who leads the way with contrast, size, shapes, color, and repetitions. A high level of complexity with a low level of visibility, reducing all effort with a careful design based on observation, testing, and iteration.

The experience, which is the way we interact with the world around us as human beings, is the journey. As

UX designers, we are not solving the user's problem, we are taking him by the hand through the path that leads to the solution. We are helping him save time and providing an enjoyable moment throughout the process. We craft the ease and satisfaction the user feels when getting to his objective.

The best UX Design goes unnoticed. And that is the beauty of it.

What Is UX?

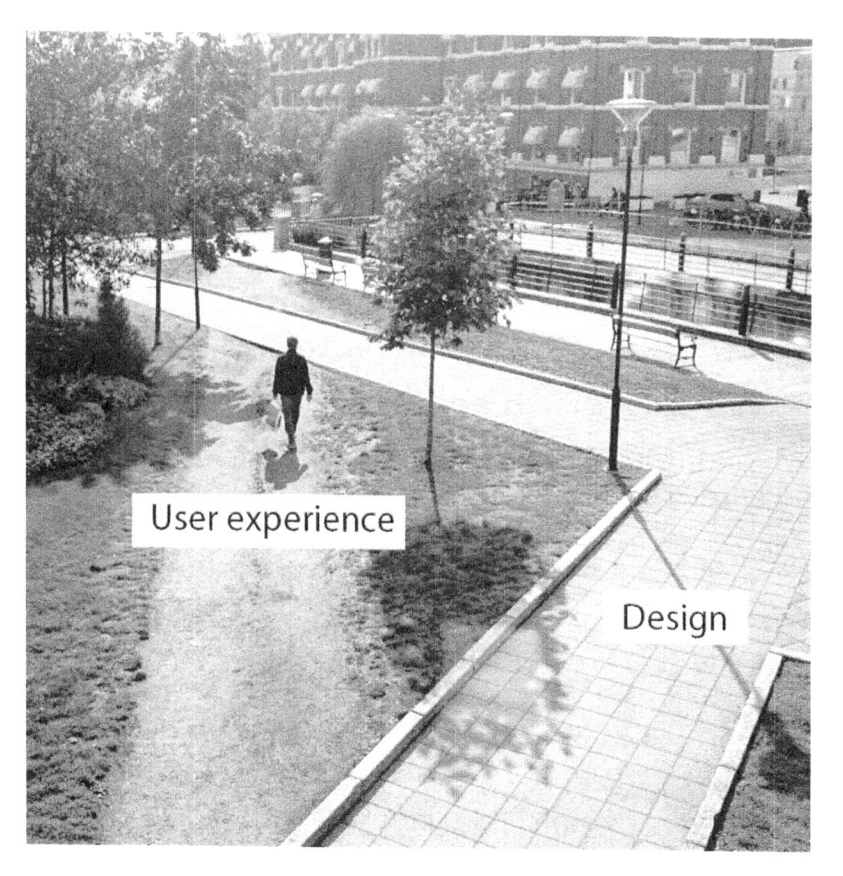

A pedestrian cutting through the grass instead of using the paved path.

What Is Design

Design is the process of visualizing and planning the creation of objects, systems, vehicles, services, spaces, buildings, etc. Its goal is to address a problem or need and provide a solution to it. That is why it is a very broad concept permeating many branches and specialties like sound design, yacht design, interior design, graphic design, and so on.

Design stands at the crossroad of science and art. Like art, it is a creative process that leads to craft beautiful items, tools, or experiences. But design is also a technical discipline approached in a comprehensive and systemic way. Its ultimate purpose is turning ideas into concrete solutions. The process starts with extensive research, collecting information, formulating a general hypothesis, and then validating it.

To put it simply, I will borrow a great definition given by fellow UX designer José Luis Antúnez: Design is nothing else than the art of crafting beautiful solutions.

As designers, we solve specific problems to meet the specific needs of users, products, businesses, and we do it with the one secret ingredient that makes everything enjoyable: beauty. We shape useful solutions in pleasant packages in order to make life easier for people.

UX Is for User Experience

User experience, or UX, can be defined as any interaction a person has with a service or a product. How the user feels, how the user navigates, and how he accomplishes his desired task. Each and every element of the interaction is taken into account by UX design. You can apply this to everything, really. From the physical book or kindle reader, you are reading these lines on, to the handle you pushed to enter the very room you are in. The size of the book, the spacing of the lines, the brightness of the screen, the shape of the handle. The goal of UX Design is to bring to the user all-round, easy, relevant, efficient, and delightful experiences.

Experience is the relationship with other humans or entities like brands, too.

Think of when you go to your favorite grocery store. You want to buy a product, you walk down the aisles (how are they spaced?), music is playing (what kind of music and why?), you look to the shelf (is it made of wood? metal? plastic?), you then interact with a cashier and walk away. Everything in this simple and trivial process is experience. You've interacted with a whole brand, colors, feelings, music, arrangements, product curation, workers, and we could go on and on. Everything is experience, everything is interface. A node on the web.

As the great Don Norman once said:

> "User experience encompasses all aspects of the end-users interaction with the company, its services, and its products."
>
> – Don Norman

UX Is for the People

While often bypassed, there's a question every designer should ask himself when approaching a project: who is this for?

This is even more true for UX designers. The end goal is to make people's life easy. Therefore, the entire process should be centered around the user, or, even better, around the person.

It is easy to fall into what I like to call the "recognition trap." Designers, like everyone else, crave to be valued and appreciated by their peers, this is why we often see talented designers slipping into making things just because they look cool, because they follow a trend or because they want to be seen as more creative than their fellows. This bias leads designers to design for designers, and not for users. As a consequence, design gets masturbatory and serves no precise purpose, losing meaning.

To prevent these tempting deviations, UX designers should always think of the user they are working for. Yes, the user. Because even if we want to be appreciated, and even if our paycheck comes from some company, the real bosses here are users.

Ask yourself, what are their needs? What are they going to do with our product? What are their behaviors, what is their background, what level of computer literacy do they have? In what context will the product be used? When, where, how?

Whatever you design, always think of the people who will use the product or service you are working on. The real people, with everything that goes with it. They are humans, just like you, not some sort of abstract user. Do you use apps or products for the sake of it? Or do you use them to fulfill a specific need? Always remember that in the end, your product is just a mere tool to help people reach their goals.

Real goals, real people. I can't stress this concept enough. You are designing new, beautiful solutions tailor-made to suit real people's needs in real life.

A useful tool to keep at hand is the so-called Job To Be Done framework. As simple as it may seem, it is the best tool I've ever used to keep this real people-concept in mind at every stage of the process.

When _____ , I want to _____ , so I can _____ .

Fill the blank spaces right at the start of the process, write it down on a Post-it note, and stick it to your whiteboard. It will help you identifying real-life user journeys or maps and come up with relevant solutions.

UX Design is for the people. Keep it in mind, and you'll be sure that your design will be a success because you've kept people at the heart of the process.

UX Is Everywhere

"Design is everywhere. From the dress you're wearing to the smartphone you're holding, it's design."

– Samadara Ginige

While many think of it that way, UX Design is not limited to the digital realm, but instead, it embraces everything we use in our daily life.

UX Design really is everywhere: the look and feel of a mobile app, the ergonomics of a vehicle, the layout of a supermarket, the wayfinding system of an airport, the toothbrush, the telephone customer service of a car rental, the handle of your oven, even language if you look carefully.

Everything is designed for human use since the dawn of time. We can go back as far as the invention of the wheel, or the design of bone arrowheads.

Every tool that has ever been invented has been perfected through testing to better suit our needs and give us, as human beings, the better user experience possible.

Think of something as simple as a hand-brush, or a toothbrush for all that matters. A chair or a sofa. A shoelace or a zip. If the item you use doesn't come easy and ends up making you spend more time than you think it deserves on it, will you still use it just because it looks good?

I've got a super cool jacket in my closet, do you know why it is still hanged in that closet right there and why I am not wearing it? It is excessively heavy for spring and too light for winter, that's why. And I bet you've had a similar experience at least once your lifetime.

As you can see, UX Design is critical to the success of a product. For good or bad...

Here are some examples of bad UX design. Hang on!

Woody and Buzz Lightyear saying "bad UX everywhere".

A nice-looking mug with pointy ears that pierce your eyes when you drink.

A Cycling path interrupted by a guardrail.

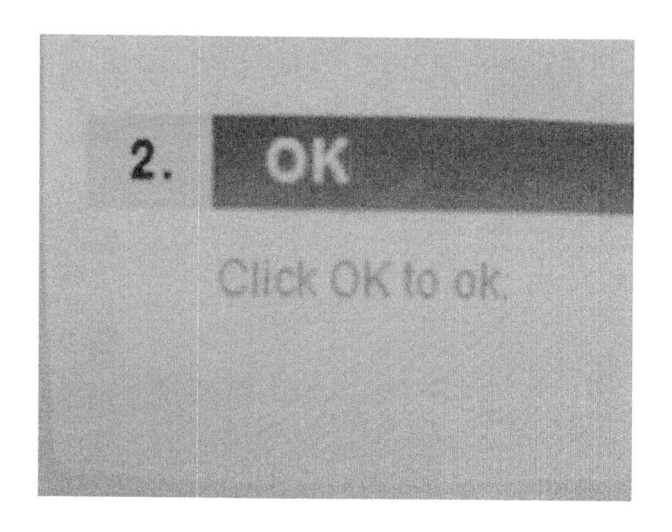

An Ok button asking user to click ok to ok.

A road drain cover built uphill so water can't flow to it.

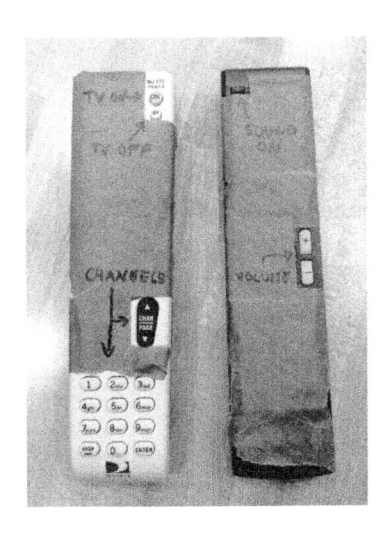

A remote tv controller with to many buttons taped to reveal only essential ones.

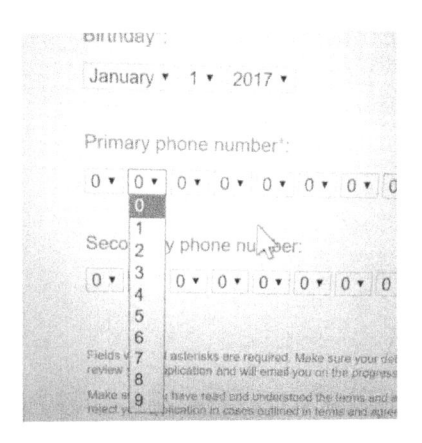

An interface forcing user to insert phone number with a dropdown for each digit.

An unintelligible elevator panel asks to push One to get to second and third floors.

An unattainable ATM seemingly built for giants.

A street crossing access for wheelchairs, but the crossing is interrupted by a second sidewalk.

A Brief History of UX

The term "user experience" has been coined by designer and psychologist Don Norman in the 90s, but can we say UX Design was born there? Of course not.

We already covered how the basic concept can be traced back to the stone age, but I want to take a little historical detour to give a broader context to this crucial field. Knowing the origins of a phenomenon always helps us navigate the present and the future.

Is it inside a mobile app, in a canoe or in a house, space has always played a fundamental role in our lives. Feng Shui is an ancient Chinese philosophy dating back to 4.000 BC and regards the spacial arrangement of objects like furniture in relation to energy and flow. It is aimed to reach harmony and practicality and concerns everything from colors to shapes and materials (beautiful solutions, anyone?).

A few thousand years later, the Ancient Greeks came up with the first ergonomic principles. They gave birth to a discipline whose ultimate goal is to understand the interactions between people and objects and between people and people. They built systems around these principles, shaping the preferred ways professions should be practiced, methods to optimize human well-being, and even inventing advanced political systems merging ergonomics, ethics, and efficiency tenets. Sounds a lot like User Experience, right?

Let's take a big jump to the early 1900s. The widely famous Taylorism gave itself the mission to enhance the efficiency of human labor by carefully designing every single aspect of the production process. Each human action, each tool, each machine was part of one big picture where every interaction was well planned. Warning: I am not stating that this was good UX. But it was indeed an attempt to shape the overall production system and experience.

In the 40s, Japanese firm Toyota (which slogan is "Always a better way" by the way) took Taylorism to a whole new level, introducing the human factor to the production system. Respect for the people and attention to their needs was the key to creating an optimal working environment. Moreover, Toyota had put in place a system in which human feedback where highly encouraged to seek constant improvement of the processes. Human behavior, testing, feedback? We're getting closer and closer!

Then came the post-war era with the electrical appliances tsunami that revolutionizes the way people lived in their daily lives. Usability applied to technology became the key factor in acquiring more customers, and Henri Dreyfuss was a pioneer in the field, improving the user experience of typewriters, tabletop telephones, and vacuum cleaners. In fact, Dreyfuss was the author of the masterpiece Designing for People, where user experience is not mentioned but permeates every word:

"When the point of contact between the product and the people becomes a point of friction, then the [designer] has failed. On the other hand, if people are made safer, more comfortable, more eager to purchase, more efficient—or just plain happier —by contact with the product, then the designer has succeeded."

– Henri Dreyfuss

The 70s witnessed psychologists and engineers come together to work on the user experience. A movement that started with Xerox and found its apogee in Apple, which introduced graphical interfaces, ease of use, typography, and even a first attempt to build an emotional relationship between people and personal computers.

And here we are, 1995, the legendary Don Norman gives UX Design its name. Norman was a cognitive scientist and the first-ever User Experience Architect at Apple. I think that leaving it to him is much better than trying to paraphrase the words of a giant like him:

"I invented the term because I thought human interface and usability were too narrow: I wanted to cover all aspects of the person's experience with a system, including industrial design, graphics, the interface, the physical interaction, and the manual."

– Don Norman

What Is UX for?

UX for Interfaces

User experience design is mostly known for its application to interfaces, is often confused with user interface design. We already covered the differences between the two, but it is always important to remember that UX and UI designers work together to ensure a smooth digital experience for the user. When it comes to digital interfaces, UX designers work on a vast array of projects included, but not limited to, smartphones, tablets, websites, mobile apps, software interfaces, CRM, email clients, management software, ATMs, e-commerce, payment terminal, digital signage kiosk, interactive maps.

UX for Products

User experience is the core concept that should guide the design process of every product. In the previous chapter, we've seen some examples of terrible design, and that should have made a case for UX design. Don Norman's masterpiece The Design of Everyday Thing is a little bible when it comes to product design and usability. Normal objects are designed with the precise goal to intuitively tell us about their purpose, how they should be used, and when they are most useful. If something doesn't work as expected, we get confused and think that something is wrong. Imagine a door that you need to push to open, but that has a handle that you usually grip and pull on. Think of a teapot or a drinking glass. Think of a chair or a fork. Think of the design of a MacBook or the latest earpods. Being intuitive is essential to have a good user experience, and you need skillful UX designers to achieve it.

UX for Content

As we discussed previously in the book, user experience comprehends all aspects of the user's interaction with the company. And that does not restrict the interfaces or touchpoints we with which we interact physically. It is also about the content we engage with. UX writing and microcopy handle what is actually written on buttons, forms, menus, error pages, confirmation messages, and so on. But you can think of anything from writing or aesthetic style to the tone of voice, copywriting, content consistency, policies, guidelines, funnels, or call to actions.

Content is part of the experience. Creating a message architecture ensures the content is blended smoothly with the designs, flows, journeys, and styles in order to create a meaningful experience.

UX for Services

This is maybe one of the least known fields of application for UX design. Services are inherently abstract and often overlooked, but over the decades, the service sector has grown dramatically, and you would be surprised to know how heavily we rely on services in our daily life. Think of call centers, customer services, check-ins, providers of any genre. Products and interfaces are really just the tips of the iceberg.

This is where UX Design overlaps with Service Design (SD) and Customer Experience (CX).

To get a clearer picture, we could make many examples from McDrives to the Starbucks experience, but I think the best case study is public transport.

User experience applied to services embraces every aspect of complex systems. The design of the busses and trains, how wide the aisles are, how many seats and standing room, accesses for wheelchairs, the routes and frequency based on the demand, the location of ticket offices and bus stops to efficiently intercept the flows. Will tickets be bought from specific offices, via smartphone, directly on the bus? Will there be an app to help users navigate the lines? How and where does the data needed to map this information will be harvested?

 Each problem has to be tackled with unique UX Design solutions, and the whole packaged wrapped in a comprehensive UX Design solution, too.

UX for Spaces

Another overlooked aspect of UX Design is the user experience applied to spaces. Directions, pathways, wayfinding systems, benches, trails, roadways, ...

Think of the disposition, or proxemics of a bar, where is the counter placed, how are the tables disposed of, where is the cash register? Designing for user flows, and ease of movement helps to avoid queues and deliver a better experience. Look at the evolution of post offices, at the itineraries of Ikea with the fixed path and the shortcuts, or how museums manage spaces to guide visitors through an emotional journey.

A shining example of a brilliant user experience applied to spaces is the legendary wayfinding system at Schipol Airport in Amsterdam. Widely praised as one of the best designs in history. Access routes, parking, buildings, and piers. It is impossible to lose oneself at that airport.

The Principles

Design Thinking

Design Thinking is an approach used for practical and creative problem-solving. It refers to the cognitive, practical, and strategic processes by which design ideas are developed. While originally created for design disciplines, many of the key concepts of design thinking have been applied to a vast range of fields, including business, engineering, and architecture.

Design Thinking is fundamentally user-centric, focusing on humans, their behavior, their goals, and their needs. The social nature of human interaction, and hence design, is at the core of the process. Ambiguity and interferences are welcomed and used to evolve and enhance design projects. This leads to the redesign rule, everything should always be iterated to better reach the desired outcome.

It consists of five phases I will only briefly cover as entire books could be written, and have been written, on this topic.

Phase One is about empathizing with the user, understanding wants, needs, and objectives.

Phase Two is where the problem is defined, and the barriers and obstacles are identified.

Phase Three is dedicated to creative ideation, a crucial point where every idea is welcomed without prejudice.

Phase Four is focused on experimenting with ideas and prototyping tangible small-scaled products.

Phase Five is the final step, and it is where user testing comes, to get feedback, correct eventual flaws in the design, and take it to the market.

The 7 Golden Rules of UX Design

1. Clarity

Confusion is the enemy. Steve Krug, author of Don't Make Me Think, affirms that a confusing design will inevitably get bad responses from users.

> "As a user, I should never have to devote a millisecond of thought to whether things are clickable or not"
>
> – Steve Krug

Designers are supposed to make their design as clear as possible because, again, the end goal is to make life easier for people. They should explain things the way they want them to them, keeping the real user in mind.

2. Intuition

Good UX Design taps into the previous pieces of knowledge and acquired references of the user. This allows users to interact with the product without any conscious reasoning.

"The main thing in our design is that we have to make things intuitively obvious"

– Steve Jobs

To be intuitive, our design should recall past user experiences with similar physical or cultural patterns. This means that different user's backgrounds can affect the feeling that a design is intuitive or not. Therefore, good UX research is key to defining who our product's user will be, which is essential to make our UX Design intuitive.

3. Digestibility

Good design is easy to digest. The quantity of energy required to interact with the product should never exceed the amount expected by the user to accomplish their objective. If your user is required to read a 500-pages manual to "get it," you're on the wrong path. Again, go back and think of yourself. Would you be willing to read through that manual, or is it too much of an entry barrier?

As a UX designer, your duty is to deliver only the necessary content at the right time. Mapping the customer journey and dividing the content in easily digestible chunks is the way.

4. Flow

User flows is often considered a tool in the UX industry, but I personally think it is much more than that. Keeping in mind how a user experience flows through its journey during the design process is, in my experience, one of the fundamental principles that should guide the designer.

Flows are a conversation that consists of the touchpoints within a system and how a user can navigate them. As designers, we should craft processes and visual clues that lead the user throughout the layout, guiding the eye from element to element with ease. This is true with the interface design, the information architecture, and with the content too. Flow is not only visual, but it is also verbal. Remember that you are building a conversation. Text pieces should not feel separated chunks but should flow as when you are talking with a real person.

5. Familiarity

Flashy design and innovative buttons might look cool on Dribbble, but if no one is clicking them, well, you've got a problem. UX designers are not here to design for designers. They are here to deliver smooth experiences to help users reach their desired outcomes. The use of familiar icons, patterns, and styles does not make you a less able designer. Systems exist for a reason. They serve to make people's lives easier, saving brain energy to be used to deal with more important tasks. Never pretend your icon is more than just an icon to your user. Of course, innovation is still possible, encouraged even, but it should be tested for real life, and on actual devices.

6. Delight

You are delighted when things work out just as expected or better than expected. That's why I found pleasure solving equations in high school. That's why kids love to throw stones in a pond, and that's why "Satisfying videos" are taking over the internet.

Satisfaction can be found in aesthetics, but only if the aesthetics serves a greater purpose and does not come in the way of the user when it comes to actually achieve their goal.

Good UX Design always aims to delight users, crafting a complex system that brings satisfaction in every aspect of the process.

7. Feedback

In the physical and digital realm, things are the same. When you make an action, you expect something to happen. Otherwise, you either think the item is not working or that you've got something wrong.

Trying to fill my online tax returns a few days ago, I was asked to upload a document. I did, but then my document won't appear anywhere. No icon, no message, nothing. I had to take my phone and call customer service. This is bad design (very bad considering the implications of a mistake in tax returns).

Users should always get feedback from their actions, success or error message when filling a form, a little animation or status change when pressing a button, and so on.

Your Perspective VS User Perspective

You are the designer, so you know perfectly what purpose a button, page, or handle actually serves. But that is because you've come up with it. Users are not you. They haven't thought about the problem to solve. They haven't been part of the creative process that led to your brilliant idea. Users expect a solution that works for them, not for you.

Most of the designers out there tend to consider themselves when designing a product, and that is where the fundamental error lies. A UX designer should take the user perspective. Always. What you like and what you come easy with is probably not what the user likes or comes easy with.

To deliver good UX designs, you have to think about what your users want and need, what are their background and abilities, what they like, what they expect. Using a user-centered approach is key to achieve user experiences that make people smile.

Design for Real Life

Designing for real life is more than a principle, it is a commandment that should be carved in stone. As a designer, it is easy to fall into the laboratory bias, thinking that what you are working on with your team in the office, using simulators and personas, is actually real. Sadly enough, it is not.

The importance of testing your products in a real-life environment, whether they are physical or digital, can't ever be stressed enough.

Thanks to testing, you can measure how your product behaves through time, where it succeeds, where it fails, what your users get immediately, what they stumble upon, where, when, and why they give up. Usability testing ensures user satisfaction, allow you to get real user reactions and feedback, usually helps spark new ideas and developing new features you had not thought about, match business decisions to real-world use and save tons of money.

Jeff Bezos, founder of Amazon, one of the most successful entrepreneurs of the century, and the wealthiest living person, investing in usability design and testing, ultimately led to Amazon's overwhelming success. In fact, according to Forbes, Amazon invested in usability testing 100 times more than in marketing in its first year.

Usability Testing is the most effective way to uncover problems and avoid putting out a product that is not working and will fail the market test. Hence, ensuring that a product is engaging, memorable, and satisfying to the user has a significant ROI, and every business should invest more in it.

Focus on the Solutions

User experience is the whole process of the user interacting with your product and every action or emotion that revolves around it. But, again, the ultimate goal is to solve a user's problem, coming up with a beautiful, easy solution.

Many out there wrongly focuses on the many features of their products, how beautiful they are, how many gigabytes they have, the materials they are made of, etc. Let's be honest. No one out there buys anything based on these pieces of information. You'll never use an uncomfortable spoon just because it looks cool or because it is made of the finest material.

As UX designers, we need to have a double approach: problem-driven and solution-based. Define the issue, provide the easiest solution. Think of Apple earpods. Earphone cables were annoying everyone, so they created cable-less earphones. Nobody cares about their color as long as they don't fall off your ears, and the sound is good, right?

Key Concepts To Keep in Mind

User Experience design encompasses much more than the look and feel of a product. It is the crossroad of many different fields, one of which is cognitive psychology. I will not cover here the many interesting finds and studies on the topic. Still, I highly recommend anyone interested in UX to delve into psychology, as there has been a significant rise in in-depth psychological knowledge in the UX job openings in the last years.

Limited User Attention

When designing a user experience, it is crucial to take into account the scarcity of attention. Our brains receive 11 million bits of data per second when human beings are only able to process 50 bits per second. It's physically impossible to pay attention to everything. Here's where inattention blindness comes in. The user's brain goes on autopilot and only sees what is relevant to it. Entire pieces of the interface or product go unnoticed even if they are right in front of the user's eye.

This is important information to keep in mind throughout the design process. To avoid it, only provide customers with what they need (If you design a job board, customers ultimately just want to get hired, if you design a teapot, customers ultimately just want to have a cup of tea), and ensure your interface is easy to scan.

Limited User Memory of the Process

As a UX designer, it is key you get familiar with the concept of working memory. It is a cognitive system in our brain that holds information temporarily. It is like the RAM of our computers, they are used to process information, but they empty when the task is done. For example, when making equations like $(25 + 37)/2$, you are using your working memory to actually do the operation and retain the numbers you've calculated to obtain the solution. Information in working memory has a short duration, something like 10-15 seconds (unless it is actively rehearsed) and has a storage capacity of 5-7 "elements" or "chunks" of information.

How much is your design taking up?

As UX designers, our duty is to reduce cognitive loads. Users' working memory has a limited capacity and duration, and part of it is probably already occupied by other activities like, say, driving. These 5-7 precious memory spots are far too precious for our brain to dedicate them extensively to the app or product we are designing. The easiest workaround is to trigger the information already stored in long-term memory, crafting simple, intuitive, and familiar designs. Don't over-deliver, keep your design quiet, and use a chunking strategy delivering the right content at just the right time.

The Design Process

Now it's time to dig a little deeper. In this chapter, I'm going to focus on the process of UX Design, which, you will learn, is an extremely varied, multifaceted field. We're going to go step by step through the whole process, from goal definition to launch, analyzing the different challenges that UX designers have to overcome to bring the original idea to life.

The following aims to be a step-by-step guide of the user experience design process to give you a taste of what is involved if you're approaching UX for the first time, or a useful blueprint that is always good to have at hand if you're already well-acquainted with what UX Design is.

Let's go!

1. Goal Definition and Problem Setting

> "Begin with the end in mind"
>
> – Stephen Covey

Goal definition is essential to every project. If you don't know where you're going, how could you ever reach your destination?

> "The trouble with not having a goal is that you can spend your life running up and down the field and never score" – Bill Copeland

When talking about user experience, there are two kinds of goals that should be defined: the business goal and the user goal.

- **Business goal**

When defining business goals, interviews have to be done with all the stakeholders in order to clearly understand what the company or companies involved want to achieve. The interviews should result in a clear problem statement, which is the first milestone needed to build a successful product.

A problem statement is a clear description of the issue that needs to be addressed. It includes a vision, an issue statement, and a method to solve the problem. It is crucial to center and focus on the team.

For example, a business may want to reach new target customers or may want to digitize its services or address some usability problems with an already existing product. Whatever the matter, it all comes down to a handful of questions:

What business problem are we trying to solve?

What is the design challenge associated with that specific problem?

UX designers, together with the stakeholders and design team, need to assess the true problem, evaluate if the goal is actually realistic, and if the direction chosen by executives actually enables the company to solve its problem and reach its goal.

I usually use the glorious 5 W's method to define:

Who does the problem affect?

In a company, the Who refers to the different sectors, like human resources or marketing, or the different business challenges, like lead generation or distribution.

What are the boundaries of the problem, what impact is it causing, what would happen if the problem is not fixed, what would happen if it does get fixed?

When does the problem occur?

The issue can be occurring at certain times of the year, or of the production process.

Where does it occur?

The problem can be occurring in certain locations, products, processes, countries...

Why does the problem occur, why it is important to fix it?

These five simple questions may seem easy to ask, but I can assure that answering them is a long and difficult process. Each answer should be as specific as possible and completely honest. Do not rush through this step of the process, because:

> "A goal properly set is halfway reached"
>
> – Zig Ziglar

- **User goal**

Companies are much more focused on their business goals and far less interested in the actual user needs. That's where the UX designer vision should intervene to recenter the discussion around what people actually need, and how the business goals can meet the user goals.

An argument for it that is usually well accepted by executives is that this is a necessary step to maximize resource use and decrease the risk of failure, in addition to reducing friction between team members in the subsequent phases. Therefore, it saves time and money.

Problem statement and goal definition processes have to be conducted for the user equally as for the business, it's like the two faces of the same coin. If business goals tend to focus on a checkout page that converts, user goals should aim to solve a real problem in the user's life. It's easier said than done, lucky enough we designers have perfected a simple strategy to the rescue: using verbs. Instead of using nouns that describe solutions, the best way to keep the mind focused on the user's need is to use verbs that represent goals and end states. For example, users don't need a dashboard (noun), they need to digest information in one place (verb). The purpose of UX Design is not to create features, but to provide an optimal solution to a user's need. We are not yet deciding on the solution. Do not bound yourself, you are just at the beginning of the process.

The desired outcome of this step of the process is a clear statement that includes a user, a need to address, and a goal. This statement will be the compass to navigate the whole process ahead of you. It is essential to align the team's vision towards a goal that is crystal clear, to help make an effective benchmark analysis, and be sure to capture actual user needs. Remember, we are not defining a solution yet. We're crafting a guide for future design decisions, but we don't want to bridle creativity. Keep it broad, without references to specific technical solutions.

Again, problem statement and goal definition are the foundation for our design process. They are absolutely essential. And if you're not convinced yet, then trust uncle Albert:

> "If I had an hour to solve a problem, I'd spend 55 minutes thinking about the problem and 5 minutes thinking about solutions"
>
> -- Albert Einstein

2. User Research

When the problem and goal are well defined, it's time to dig into User Research.

Each UX Design project starts with User Research, it is every UXer's starting point, as it helps us learn more about the users, their goals and motivations, their needs, and behaviors.

User research is essential to the UX Design process. I would even say that UX Design would not even exist without User Research. Without it, we wouldn't be able to learn about how users actually interact and navigate our system, and we wouldn't be able to identify the obstacles they find in their way to their goal.

Under no circumstances should you skip this process. It's the backbone of everything related to user experience. You cannot afford to overlook this part of the process. And your clients neither, whether they realize it or not.

Skipping User Research is a common pitfall onto which executives stumble upon when they think they know everything about users because hey, that's obvious, right? Everything wants this or that!

Please, please, please do not pretend to know your users before having done proper research. UX isn't marketing. And even in marketing, one should do extensive research if they want to avoid throwing money out the window. But we'll leave that to marketing experts. We're busy enough here with our UX process.

Remember that what you (or the executives) think is intuitive, probably won't work for actual users. The purpose of User Research is just about that. Finding out what real users really need. And as you can imagine, it is critical to the success of your design.

"Research is worth nothing if you don't act on it properly. The leap between research insight and the design action is the most important part of a UX designer's job"

– Harry Brignull, UX consultant

As a UX designer, you are the expert for your product. But experts are experts because they know it all about their business, not because they brag around.

Assumptions are the worst enemy of every UX designer. And every product, too.

To do User Research properly, you have to get rid of them first. When working with assumptions, we fail to notice what the experience could be like for other users. We are heavily influenced by our own experience, and this tends to leave us blind to other people's experiences. That's what you would try to avoid. Not only because you risk to miss out huge opportunities, but because your whole process would be flawed.

What you find obvious to navigate, is influenced by your background story, and by the fact that you are working on it, so you already know the steps to reach the goal.

Users don't have this privilege. They will have to find their way alone in the layout and do not know what to expect before they actually try it.

This is why User Research is so important to the UX Design process.

Recall the principles: a UX designer's job is to make people's life easy. You are the advocate for them, and should always think from their perspective. And the only way to learn about that perspective is by performing in-depth User Research with real users. There are no shortcuts.

As every foundation, User Research has to come first in the UX Design process, otherwise, assumptions will take the lead. It provides the data we need to proceed into further steps of the design process. Without those, we can't advance, we can't build any product.

Doing research later on only results in a waste of time, work, resources, and money. A necessity for huge adjustments and redesign will emerge to fit that very user needs you should have had right from the start.

In fact, User Research helps us identify precisely how our target users move and feel when interacting with products designed to meet their desired outcome. The research stage gathers important information from diverse sources and contexts to provide a deeper understanding of the potential user to UX designers.

As we are trying to wear the user's shoes, there's a fundamental muscle UX designers, and researchers must learn to flex: empathy. When conducting research you'll be working with many different persons with a great variety of backgrounds. You must not judge them, but rather your job is to understand them and why they are behaving the way they do. You must not try to orientate their actions or influence their behavior. Just listen to them and observe them. Be careful not to fall in the confirmation bias. It could be deadly for your product.

Remember, UX is a mindset. It is a commitment to watch the world through the user's eyes, and make sure that everything is made to serve them in the way they need to be served.

There is a handful of mindset tips I want to share with you.

Many beginners do a lot of listening and underestimate the observation part. But many of our actions are. Guided by unconscious patterns and often people are not aware of the, By combining observation and a good knowledge of psychology, UX designers can learn more than when they just ask the user.

Newbies also often take the process too rigidly without the necessary space for interpretation. But the true power of the User Research process and tools is unleashed when UX designers allow themselves to think outside the box. That doesn't mean burning the rules and dancing over their corpses, but rather being creative with the tools and methodologies provided by the UX toolkit. Creativity is not limited to the design step, research needs it just as much. Each new product, each new experience that you craft has unique peculiarities, and a different user base. Be creative with the way you conduct interviews and research. Find new ways to collaborate with your team. UX is about the experience, not cold useless data.

    No boundaries ahead. Yes, User Research has to be conducted at the beginning of the process, but repeating it is not forbidden. With the advancement of technology, UX designers are given a chance to conduct research more frequently, more cheaply, and more consistently. We can build a framework where continuous feedback is the rule. Where the conversation with the user never stops. UX Design is iterative by definition, it's up to you to build a loop of product design and development. Embrace the -"always in beta" state of mind, and with little effort and resources, you will be able to fine-tune your product and stay relevant to your user by reinforcing your foundations.

> "Good user research is key to designing a great user experience. Designing without good user research is like building a house without solid foundations— your design will soon start to crumble and will eventually fall apart"
>
> – Neil Turner, founder of UXfortheMasses

Now it's time to look at the most common tools to conduct good User Research.

The Research Learning Spiral

The Research Learning Spiral, created by Erin Sanders, a senior interaction designer, and design researcher, provides a framework of five main steps for conducting good UX research. Step one and step two are about forming questions and hypotheses. Step three, four, and five instead, are about collecting knowledge via selected User Research methods.

According to Sanders, the Spiral has been created to help designers answer questions and overcome obstacles, especially when they struggle to choose what direction to take in the different design phases. It is a process of learning and need-finding.

Let's take a look at those five steps:

1. Objectives: What are the knowledge gaps we need to fill?

2. Hypotheses: What do we think we understand about our users?

3. Methods: Based on time and manpower, what methods should we select?

4. Conduct: Gather data through the selected methods.

5. Synthesize: Fill in the knowledge gaps, prove or disprove our hypotheses, and discover opportunities for our design efforts.

Let's explore each step a little deeper.

1. *Objectives: The questions we are trying to answer*

Gather your team, then start by discussing what you already know about the product's goal. I usually find it useful to write a series of framing questions down on paper or sticky notes and arrange them onto a table or board. This speeds up the process and helps to keep the team focused.

The aforementioned questions should be written in the 5Ws + 1H form. Note that you can have multiple questions with the same W or H.

- The Who helps you define who the target audience is, pinpointing their demographics and other key information.

- The What clarifies what products, apps, or features potential users are already using to solve their needs.

- The When determines when in time people might be using the products identified in by the What. It also helps to determine what routines or sets of behavior that actions occur. An important step to explore the person behind the user.

- The Where helps to define the physical context in which potential users usually perform the tasks you are targeting. Some technologies or products might be bound at certain places (think ATMs), ore some specific websites.

- The Why is key to explain what motivates the potential user. At this point, you explore the hidden drivers of their actions and decisions, whether they are rational or emotional, conscious, or unconscious.

- The How helps you dig into detail on the different steps and actions your targeted users have to perform in order to fulfill their needs.

In not more than an hour or two, you will be able to come up with a variety of framing questions that bring you forward in your research. You can now proceed with the debate, choosing which questions to prioritize, narrowing the focus, and going lateral. The outcome should then be translated into research objectives (that are not questions, but rather statements) that will serve as guidelines for your team's research efforts, and to select the right tools and methods for your specific needs. Always try to find a balance. Not too tight, not too broad.

2. *Hypotheses: what we believe we already know*

This may be the trickiest step. It is where assumptions come to you, whispering at your ear. You've got intuitions about the possible solutions, and clients too. Why not going ahead and execute them hands-on?

We've all been through this. Early ideas always seem perfect, and intimately we like to think we're geniuses coming up with brilliant ideas right away. I'm not a stranger to this either. But as UX designers, the ego is an obstacle.

Instead, try formulating hypotheses and watch ideas as prompts shouted by someone else. Externalizing your hypotheses, you'll find more awareness on their true merits, and you'll be able to minimize the influence of yours and the client's biases. This usually helps me gain clarity and select the right methods to factor my research plan.

In fact, taking hypotheses for what they are and not mistaking them for proven solutions is the best way to communicate your findings throughout the process with your team, and with executives. "We believed this, but we discovered that instead."

There are three kinds of hypotheses you can possibly formulate:

- Attitude-related hypotheses: what do your users like to do?
- Feature-related hypotheses: what feature users are more likely to use?
- Behavior-related hypotheses: what do users want to achieve and what they do to achieve it?

Write down or sketch out each hypothesis you generate with your team, this again will help you reduce your cognitive load and stay focused on the task.

3. Methods: how we plan to fill the gaps in our knowledge

If the previous steps are well-conducted, the methods step is fairly straight-forward. Once you have your research objectives and hypotheses at hand, it's time to consider which methods are the best fit to reach your specific goal.

Research methods could be divided into three categories. There is not an absolute best one, it's up to you to understand which one or which ones (since you can combine them) are the most appropriate to your needs.

- **Building a foundation**

Methods in this category include observational interviews, contextual interviews, card sorting, surveys, market analysis, and trend exploration.

When to use these methods: when you don't have a sufficient understanding of the users you are designing for, or when a user base is fluid.

- **Generating ideas**

Methods in this category include diary studies, paper prototyping, card sorting again, and other participatory design activities such as collages, co-creating sketches, diagrams, and rough interface examples.

When to use these methods: when you already have a good understanding of the people who will be using your product, and you want to gather feedback on some ideas and design hypotheses you've formulated.

- **Evaluating design**

Methods in this category include paper prototyping, usability testing, cognitive walkthrough, and heuristic evaluations.

When to use these methods: when you need to clarify how people want to. Use. The product to achieve its objective. They help to refine your prototypes, whether they are about the design, the code, or real-life simulations.

Are you feeling overwhelmed by the number of methods listed? Fear not, for we'll delve deeper into the different methods in a moment.

4. Conduct: gather data through the methods we've selected

Once the research plan is done, the hypotheses are set, and the methods identified, it's time to conduct research!

Go into the field and recruit a dozen people. Try to schedule the meetings based and the when and where questions from the first step. Prepare an interview guide with questions and stimuli, and before putting it into practice, test it with coworkers, so you'll be able to refine it before diving into the actual interview.

Research sessions put you in front of real people that most likely have a different background from you. That's where empathy should take the lead. Do not judge people, but rather facilitate sessions by capturing the events through notes, videos, photos, and any kind of useful material.

Your sessions may change over time, it is perfectly normal.

> "You wouldn't be learning if you didn't have to shift at least a little bit"
>
> – Lauren Serota, associate creative director at Frog

Always ask yourself if the process is helping you discover what you need. If it isn't, chances are you've committed some errors. Correcting them and shifting methods or approaches is a sign of wisdom.

You could think that if you're not learning anything new but only confirming information that you already know, it's because, in the end, you were right, and thus you can stop the research and move on. It may be. Anyone who's telling you it is impossible is not telling you the truth. It is indeed possible that you have conducted the perfect analysis, and already found the solution. It is possible, but it is unlikely. It only occurred to me two times in my career. Most of the time, my team and I had to find out some major or minor mistakes regarding the recruiting and definition of our target audience, flaws in our hypotheses or, an evaluation error when choosing the appropriate method.

Always balance research sessions with analysis. This way, you'll be able to adjust and adapt to the findings, and you'll save time, money, and resources.

5. *Synthesize: answer our research questions, and prove or disprove our hypotheses*

Now that you've gathered research data, it's time to summarize your findings and answer your research questions.

This is often a messy process. You've ended up with a bunch of data, and now your job is to find meaning in it. As we already discussed before in this book, be careful not to rely solely on cold data. Most of our behaviors are dictated by subconscious activity. Therefore a dose of interpretation is needed. Read between the lines, rewatch videos to search for clues, look at the body language, and so on. Your goal here should be to find the why behind the data.

The more meaning you are able to extract from your research data, the more effective the design process will be. So, you would always want to snatch more time to go through this part.

The outcome of this step of the process should be the assembly of clear, terse, actionable findings into a one-page document. You can, of course, attach the whole research bundle, but the operational document should be concise and straight to the point. It should provide the answers to your research objectives, point at which hypotheses have been proved or disproved, what patterns have been found that the design should take advantage of, what is more important to the user, and what are the overall implications of the product you're designing.

As a result, your team will become more confident and have a rock-solid foundation to advance into the design process.

User Groups

Tools and methods, here we are. User groups are structured interviews conducted to reveal the desires and needs of a target audience. They constitute a widely used method, also known outside the UX realm as "focus groups." They are often inexpensive and provide a lot of insight without taking that much time to conduct, and they are usually a good starting point for research. User groups are a great tool, but they are not self-sufficient, they don't provide an accurate measurement of behavior, and always need to be combined with other methods and tools to deepen the research.

"It's really hard to design products by user groups. A lot of times, people don't know what they want until you show it to them"

– Steve Jobs

What people say, think, feel, and do are often very different. Moreover, the fact that user groups are conducted with multiple users at a time, people get influenced by each other, resulting in biases that can produce inaccurate data.

In any case, user groups are a useful method to help you better understand how users perceive a product, what are the most important features in their opinion, what are the issues they experience while interacting with the product, how and why the product fails to meet their expectations.

Gathering this kind of information, user groups have proven to be also helpful in generating new business and design ideas.

Some best practices for conducting user groups go from asking good, clear, open-ended questions, restricting the topics investigated, and including the right number of participants to allow everyone to speak and ensure enough variety in the approach to the product.

 Be sure to take notes and record the session. Establishing roles among your team, based on a precise schedule, and discussion guide is also critical to achieving good results during user groups. Be as precise as you can, choose who is going to moderate, who will drive the discussion, how deep the questions would be, etc.

User Interviews

User interviews are. Fundamentally different from user groups. Indeed, user interviews are in-depth one-on-one discussions with the user. The objective is to discover the underlying needs and requirements that a user has when using your product.

Interviews can be conducted as simple discussions or while the user interacts with the product. They are one of the most employed tools because they allow UX designers to ask questions to reveal what the user is thinking or feeling as they interact with the product or service we're designing. It helps identify the greatest pain points and strengths of our design and make comparisons with other products or services the user may be used to fulfill their need. User interviews make up a powerful tool to answer the When and Where questions defined in the Objectives step of the Spiral. A one-on-one discussion is ideal ton gather information about daily routines and systems of behavior.

Some UX designers even use those interviews to get suggestions on what the ideal product looks like for the user. However, in my experience, this usually puts too much stress on the interviewees, nine out of ten indicating already existing products or features, and being fuzzy.

This kind of interview can be conducted in person, over a video, or even via voice call. They can be held at the user's home, in a lab, or in the location where your product or service is supposed to be used. For example, contextual interviews take place in the everyday environment inhabited by the user, following their movement across the day. This particular method has the advantage of providing more insights relating to the context in which your design will be used and uncover real-life flaws that you might have been overlooking.

Interviewing users is not a mere chat with people. Therefore a number of best practices have been developed through time to help UX designers achieve their research goals. These strategies are at the core of a human-centered approach. It's where the U of UX stands. Without them or similar methodologies of user research, UX would just not exist. A rigorous, well-planned approach is key to gather valuable data worth acting upon. It helps to avoid mistaking symptoms for root causes. It is essential to identify the real-life problem of the user and to understand how we UX designers can help them solve it by simplifying their lives and lowering their cognitive or physical load.

- **Don't ask leading or directed questions**

Leading questions are mom questions. "Are you hungry? Should I prepare some pancakes?". The answer is suggested. Therefore you are giving up on honest feedback and ruining the whole interview.

- **Don't ask people what they want**

Users don't know what they want. Asking them what they want is useless (remember what Steve Jobs. Had to. Say about this). They're not professional designers, they won't provide magical or innovative solutions. Your job is to understand their problem and then build fresh solutions.

- **Don't ask yes/no questions**

Avoid yes/no questions. You want expansive responses, that can get you closer to your goal, not dead-end monosyllabic feedback.

- **Ask open-ended questions**

Open-ended questions are key to finding out what issues people are struggling with and what their problems are. Ask them about how valuable to their life the product is, let them talk.

- **Don't make assumptions. Ask stupid questions.**

Assumptions are the enemy. Don't ask obvious questions you may miss relevant information. Moreover, basic questions are a great way to make people at ease.

- **Ask the same question from multiple angles**

When it comes to the heart of your interview, work your user to be sure that they really get to the core of what they think. Do not ask the same question over and over in a row, use multiple angles, and spread these questions throughout your script.

- **Ask follow-up questions**

Don't settle for whatever the interviewee says. Ask follow up questions on the topics that need further clarification.

- **Never mention other users**

"A lot of people say ...". That only triggers prejudice and fear of missing out on the user. Therefore you'll get false answers and ruin your interview.

- **Have a set of questions you use every time**

Do not go random into that good night. To have a methodologically valid interview, you should have the same base set of questions every time. Also, this is useful to fine-tune your questions and get better at interviewing people.

- **Embrace silence**

Never make small talk during the interview. Embrace awkward silences, more often than not, the participant will fill them with more information.

- **Don't be afraid of the truth**

It's not about you. It's about the product. Your job is to gather truthful information to design the best product possible. Your hypotheses are not the product, do not become attached to them. You want to know the truth. Just ask the uncomfortable questions.

- **Be neutral**

You are designing for people. Not for yourself, not for the company, not for fellow designers. Do not defend your product or client. Just listen and take note of the problems users are facing.

- **Ask users to show you**

 If the interviewee mentions something interesting that you could see, ask them to show you. Seeking to better understand is not a crime. In the end, you are doing it for them, right?

- **Record and take notes**

Take detailed notes, but if you can, record the interview as well. Audio at a minimum. Recording interviews is particularly useful to show your team or executives and help everyone work together, without prejudices.

- **Synthesize findings and make recommendations**

Raw material is good, but try to make it digest by someone other than you. Synthesize your observations, no one would ever read a one hundred page report. You are a UX designer, right?

Online Surveys

Online surveys are questionnaires submitted via the web to your target users, with a set of precise questions. Length and format can vary, but always remember that the user experience of the form is also important. Therefore, do not ask people to fill endless surveys for free. They won't complete it, or at the very least, they will rush through the last questions of your survey, contaminating your data.

Online surveys have many strengths. First of all, they are quick and inexpensive. Then, they can reach hundreds or thousands of users everywhere in the world, leveraging the power of the internet. They also are anonymous, which usually makes people feel more comfortable revealing their true thoughts and emotions.

Designing surveys, however, can be a tricky part. You should carefully balance closed and open-ended questions. Closed one gather more quantitative data and are more easily processed, while open-ended one is more likely to collect qualitative data, but usually take longer to analyze.

When it comes to writing up the questions, the same best practices as for user interviews apply. However, the medium is much more limiting here, so there's another set of best practices to take into account that is specific to online surveys:

- **Set goals**

What are you trying to learn about your user? Unfocused questionnaire results in useless data. Keep in mind the end goal of your research when crafting the questionnaire.

- **Test with pilot users**

Don't roll out the questionnaire until you've tested it. It shouldn't be a time-consuming test, but asking colleagues and coworkers to take up the survey will help you spot errors and get useful corrections. It is also your only chance to actually see someone taking that online survey. And this is invaluable.

- **Set a screener**

Skim out the audience by adding screening questions upfront. Having your survey filled by non-users will pollute your data, and can even make you take the wrong design direction.

- **Simple questions**

Keep the questions clear, use accessible language, and give appropriate context. You would not want to force users to go google about your confusing questions. Also, consider adding support in the local language where needed.

- **Keep it open**

Your questionnaire should be as open as possible. Your goal is to gather the preference, motivation, and reason for particular behaviors, states, or reactions. Therefore, you should design the form to allow users to give you this information.

- **Ask one concept at a time**

Do not mix things up. Follow the golden rule, "one concept one question." The user may not understand questions that contain more than one concept, they may skip one of the concepts, or at least be influenced by one of the concepts while answering the other. Confusing questions degrade the quality of the gathered data.

- **Be transparent**

Be honest with your users. Tell them what you are going to use their data for. Ask them if they are available sharing these details with you, and proceed only if they agree.

- **Respect your user's anonymity**

Privacy is everything online. Users might become suspicious if you ask them personal data such as name, address, or phone number. Always provide good reasons to ask them, but most of all, ask yourself about whether or not do you really need all that data for your goals.

- **Respect people's time**

Reduce the number of questions to keep only the most relevant. You don't want people to skip important questions because the length of your questionnaire is too much.

- **Organize the questions**

Structure the survey to avoid overloading the user's mind, start with simple questions, and alternate more heavy ones. Also, add segmentation to avoid giving the user that infinite survey sensation.

- **Design for conditionality**

Some questions may be conditional to certain user segments. When it occurs, it is crucial to only collect data about the target segment, so be sure to apply strategies to make unwanted users avoid those questions.

- **Balance your rating scale**

In closed questions, don't put more positive or negative options, otherwise, you could get misleading answers influenced by how you compiled the possible answers.

- **Give a way out**

Always keep in mind that the options provided might not apply to every user. Don't forget to provide a "not applicable" or open-ended option.

- **Show progress**

To reduce the chances of drop-offs, keep users informed about how long it would take to complete the questionnaire. Tell them right off the bat and use a progress bar throughout the process.

- **Going live**

Well, your questionnaire is live now. Very good, indeed. But how will you get your target users to fill it out? It is important to know how you will engage people and convince them to take up the survey.

- **Incentivize the users**

You cannot expect that people will take up the survey out of sheer generosity. Consider giving gift cards, free trials. Think about which lead magnet is most likely to motivate the user to take your questionnaire.

Card Sorting

Card sorting is one of the most used methods when it comes to Information Architecture. When a sorting session is held, designers instruct participants to organize cards in topics and categories that reflect their experience of the website, service, or product. To be more exact, as the user may never have used the product, they are asked to organize the cards in a way that makes sense to them. In a way, they expect the product to work.

It is a simple, inexpensive, and a rather quick method to gather precious information about your target users. It is a flexible tool too, you can use actual cards, mere pieces of paper, post-it notes, or even software apps.

I especially like to rely on card sorting at the very beginning of the research. Of course, it is not a self-sufficient tool, and have to be paired with other UX methods, like interviews, or early usability testing, but it helps you collect insights on how the user's mind works, revealing their thoughts on categories, grouping, and labeling. This is especially useful when you're working on a website or app project, but it also works well with vocal interfaces.

Conducting card sorting has many benefits. First of all, it helps UX designers better understand how topics are relevant to the potential audience, and what expectations users will have. This way, it makes your job easier to decide what to put on your website homepage, how to structure your app, how to label navigation and categories, and how many do you actually need. Basically, it gives you insights on how to build a journey, user flows, and information architecture of your product.

Be careful not to rely solely on this technique to gather data about users. Despite providing many advantages, it is not the best-suited tool to identify the tasks and goals of the user.

When conducting card sorting sessions, the principal activity is to ask users to organize information written on labeled cards, and sort them in logical groups. This can be achieved in two different ways and using diverse media.

- **Closed card sorting**

The UX Design team provides users with both the category cards and content cards. They are then asked to organize the content cards in the given categories in a way that makes sense to them. This method is normally used when adding new content to an existing site or gaining a second round of insights after an open card sort.

When to choose this method: when you need to add new content to existing information architecture. For me, I usually use it when conducting a second round after an open card session.

- **Open card sorting**

This time the UX Design team only provides the content cards to the users, which are then asked to organize the cards into categories by themselves. It is the user that will compose groups and categories, and it is the user that will label them in a way they find appropriate.

When to choose this method: when you're starting to build new information architectures from scratch.

This process is cheap and quick, whatever the media you choose to conduct the session. It is worth noting, though, that you can do card sorting research sessions the classic way, that is face to face, or leverage the power of the internet, and do it remotely.

- **Face to face card sorting**

As the label suggests, face to face card sorting is conducted in person. The UX designer is present and acts as a mere observer, becoming a facilitator only if needed by the participant. He encourages the user to talk through their thoughts and explaining the mental processes undergoing their decisions. This technique allows UX designers to clarify any doubt, gathering observations, and insights about the reasoning behind decisions.

- **Remote card sorting**

Remote card sorting, on the other hand, makes use of online software that allows us to set up and distribute the session to a large number of users. Participants work with their own computer, and with no conduct with the UX Design team. Upsides are that you are able to collect a much greater amount of data, targeting users all around the world at almost no cost and that the tools are usually already equipped with data analysis features that will speed up the analyzing step. Downsides are the lack of contact that prevents you from getting to know about the actual thoughts behind the choices. Software tools are Optimal Sort. These online software tools provide you with a number of ways to analyze the data. As the test is conducted remotely, there is no contact with the user, so there is no way of understanding the reasoning behind why the user has arranged the cards in a certain way.

When the session is done, it's time for UX designers to take a look at all the data collected, entering it in spreadsheets, or cluster data software to make sense of the pile. The analysis stage is a crucial one. You want to identify common trends and patterns that can give you useful. And actionable clues about how to build effective information architecture.

Personas

> "Be someone else. It takes great empathy to create a good experience. To create relevant experiences, you have to forget everything you know and design for others. Align with the expected patience, level of interest, and depth of knowledge of your users. Talk in the user's language."
>
> – Niko Nyman, senior developer, and UX designer

A user persona is a fictional representation of your ideal customer based on your User Research and should include the goals, needs, and behavior of your customer target. Personas are usually meant to represent actual potential users or customers you already have. They are the result of a creative process that is rooted in data. Many fledgling UX designers get carried away, so I think it is important to note that caution is needed. Be careful not to fill it with your desired customer. Most users aren't perfect and will struggle here and there with your product. When I say personas are ideal customers, I mean that they should meet your expected target audience, just do not lose yourself in fantasies. Instead, build user personas based on quantitative and qualitative data from your research. Remember that although these personas are a hundred percent fictional, they still have to represent a selection of the real audience you are aiming to. Otherwise, your personas will jeopardize your design.

A good user persona should represent a large portion of our desired or actual users, taking into account their goals, needs, and motivations. The objective of this tool is to give users more precise clues on what user's expectations are, making for an accurate picture of how they will interact with our products and its different features. Nevertheless, the most valuable aspect of this method, to me, is that it forces you to wear other people's shoes. It reminds UX designers why they are doing all this research and design for real people with real lives and real problems.

But let the master do the talking here:

"Portraits and profiles of user types (and their goals and behaviors) remind us all that "you are not the user" and serve as an invaluable compass for design and development."

— Peter Morville, founding father of Information Architect (and protector of us all)

This is the foundation to achieve good UX Design and good persona creation. As designers, we have to understand who will be using our product. Whether we're talking about a physical product, a wearable, a service, or a smartphone app, we have to fight the tendency to design things that meet our personal interests and expectations and focus on the user. No user, no product. It's as simple as this.

A persona is a powerful tool to get to know your users and make a product more useful to them. Therefore it should provide answers to questions like "who is our ideal customer?", "What is their pattern behavior?", "What do they consciously want?", "What do they need instead?".

This is a critical question to ask. As we mentioned before in the book, people usually think they know what they want, but they usually get trumped by external drives. Needs are on a much deeper level, and it is effectively answering them that will decide whether or not your product will be successful or a complete failure.

Well-defined personas enable UX designers to pinpoint those needs and identify the behavior that may prevent them from fulfilling them, along with the obstacles people find on their way. And once you understand the needs and goals, the obstacles, and drives, well, the ball is already rolling, and addressing them will come much easier.

Here I want to share a few best practices I've found useful in my experience as a senior UX designer.

- **Don't skip the basics**

Good user personas should contain four key pieces of information.

1. A Header, that includes a fictional name, picture, and quotes summarizing what matters to the persona.

2. A Demographic profile based on user research, including personal, professional, and user background. Try to be specific here, including the wage and field of the personas' job, the tools used at work, the environment they move into... Also,

add psychographics, depicting interests, attitudes, motivation, and pain points.

3. At least one End Goal that inspires action into the persona. It should include both goals and needs.

4. A Scenario that describes how the persona interacts with your product in its daily life. At this point, you should aim to build a "day-in-the-life" narrative, from the moment the persona wakes up, till they turn the light off. Get into the user's shoes and be broad about every activity done in the day. Your product will probably have a little space on that day, it is of the greatest importance to understand when, where, and why it would be used.

- **Make it realistic**

Avoid exaggerations, your product will be real, your user too.

- **Keep it short**

Avoid extra detail, reason on everything, but when compiling the document, focus on essential elements. Typically we don't go over than a one-page user persona document. It should be handy and actionable.

A well-defined persona is helpful throughout the whole process of researching, designing, and testing. Using a combination of tools, together with personas, is the best way to conduct user research and get to know critical information that will orient the process and influence the final design.

"Conducting user research allows you to dive deep beneath the surface of what your users say they want, to instead uncover what they actually need. It's the key to ensuring that your products and features will actually solve the problems that your clients face on a day to day basis. User research is imperative if you want to create a successful, habit-forming product."

— Jennifer Aldrich, UX and Content Strategist at InVisionApp

    Now that you've learned that to a well-conducted User Research is essential to launch a useful and usable solution for the user. Now that you've collected enough data. Now that you've analyzed it and make it into a handy readable document of a few pages. It's time to move on and start the actual design and development of your product.

3. Design and Develop

First off, a disclaimer. Most people blame UX Design, accusing it of killing creativity and resulting in outcomes that always seem to resemble each other. Is it true? Yes, but no.

UX is ultimately about solving user problems. If UX Design addresses new problems, it will find new creative solutions, but if it addresses long-standing issues, then a choice has to be made. Going for an already existing solution and make a product that is a mere additional choice in the offer. Or rather being creative, and going for an innovative solution that will position the product ahead of the competition, or possibly in a completely new market.

Sad enough, most of the businesses out there hiring UX designers are trying to elbow their way to get a piece of the existing pie. But there's a quote I want to write down in this book, for myself and everyone who will read it. It is famous, but not a banal one.

> "If I had asked people what they wanted, they would have said faster horses."
>
> — Henry Ford

Without innovation, people would still be riding horses, hunting for their food, or living in caves. But fortunately, humans have been innovating since the dawn of time, continuously improving their quality of life along the way.

Innovating UX is a natural extension of that eager to make life easier, and find creative solutions to day-to-day problems. Pledge allegiance to UX innovation! Be creative, be innovative, and you could have the opportunity to shape the world around you.

This due premise pronounced. It's time to get our hands dirty and open our design toolkit. Here's where the magic comes.

Wireframing

Wireframing is a method that helps UX designers to design digital interfaces, such as websites, mobile app, software, wearable app. How do you decide where to put images or videos? How to choose between a three or five-column grid? Will you go for pagination or infinite scroll? Vertical, horizontal, or in-depth scrolling?

To answer these questions user experience, designers use wireframes.

Wireframes are a handy tool to design an interface at a structural level. It helps define the layout with the various elements displayed on a particular page or screen. Consider it as a skeletal framework.

In fact, according to usability.gov, "A wireframe is a two-dimensional illustration of a page's interface that specifically focuses on space allocation and prioritization of content, functionalities available, and intended behaviors."

Space allocation, prioritization, and intended behavior. That's what we try to achieve with wireframes. No images, color, styling, nice little graphics or illustrations. Wireframes are not meant for visual design. They are meant to focus on key elements, functionalities, and how our target audience is going to interact with them.

Wireframing is one of the first steps in the design process. This way, it is much easier for designers to bring changes based on the feedback gathered throughout the process. No need to explain why it is critical to iterate and implement, rather than having to turn our design inside-out when we realize our final mockup is flawed, right?

Therefore, wireframes are our best ally when it comes to detecting issues early, map out functionalities, and avoid an infinite round of revisions in the final stage when every change means going through a complex and painful work.

Wireframes are essential to save time. When wireframing, designers actually lay down the blueprint that will guide the construction of the end product, adjusting and measuring the usability across the different phases of the development process, from wireframes to prototypes to the final deliverable.

Like every blueprint, wireframes force you to focus on the essential, getting rid of all unessential details such as color, images, and content. They force you to focus only on the layout and functionality of the interface, positioning each element on the page to structure information, design usability, and achieve the cleanest technical user experience. I say "technical" because UX is not only about functionality, but it's about the feelings too, as we discussed extensively in the first chapters of this book.

Wireframing usually enters the field after the user research stage, when you've gathered enough information on what needs and motivations are to your target user. Nonetheless, it can also come in handy during the discovery process if you need to explore variations or new possibilities within your design.

There are two different types of wireframes:

- **Low-Fidelity Wireframes, or Lo-Fi**

They consist of tough paper sketches, including the most basic, static content. They are used to kickstart the wireframing process and get ideas down quickly.

- **High-fidelity Wireframes, or Hi-Fi**

They consist of highly detailed layouts, with all the details usually missing from their Lo-Fi counterpart. Most advanced one can even be interactive, with some basic coding involved. Of course, it takes more time to make a Hi-Fi wireframe, and it is not recommended to start off with this kind of detail as you want to be sure to have your basic design already outlined before diving into such a time-consuming task.

Starting with pen and paper is just fine. It is quick and effective and allows you to put so many ideas on paper without having any quality standard expectation, therefore freeing your mind even more, and letting you be more creative. There are also plenty of printable pdfs for wireframing on the internet, if you prefer to have some reference device size, or prompts.

As an alternative, you can use a wide variety of digital wireframing tools that come in with pre-composed elements to drag and drop or draw on the page. It really all comes down to how you're feeling, and what tools you find yourself most comfortable with. Just to name a few, you can try Balsamiq, Invision, and MarvelApp.

Wireframing is as simple as it is essential. I would say that the UX process would be maimed without wireframing. My desk is always full of sketches where I put down my ideas. Wireframes keep my mind working on new ideas, and if I'm not satisfied with the result, I just tear off the piece of paper and grab a new one. Moreover, it is an incredibly useful tool to work with your team, communicate with stakeholders, and to share with target users or coworkers, and collect feedback at every stage of the design process.

Information Architecture

As you may have noticed, Information Architecture (IA) happens to be one of the four quadrants of UX. Therefore I think we may use some further presentations.

Information Architecture is the art, and science, of structuring and organizing content of software apps, websites, mobile apps, and similar. It consists of deciding how to arrange the different parts of something to make something understandable.

When you're loading information onto your product, you want it to be found and used. Thus, information architects' job is to make it happen. They organize content in a manner that would be easily reachable to the user, allowing them to find whatever they need effortlessly, and easily adjust to the product's features. Of course, there's no magical recipe, this content arrangement should be based on the peculiarity of each product.

UX and IA have the same overall goal, which is to make life easier for people. The fundamental difference between User Experience and Information Architecture lies in the different roles they play. While being essential to each other, they serve different purposes, like teammates on a sports team.

IA deals with the skeleton of the design. Without it, any user interface would fall apart. Unorganized content makes it difficult for the user to navigate, so they can easily get lost or feel annoyed. A bad interaction is a perfect guarantee for failure. Unless you're bringing an absolute innovation in the field, there is just too much choice out there to hope to get a second chance for your product. Again, without laying proper foundations, everything falls apart, and building a compelling user experience is extremely difficult.

IA serves as the blueprint and materials for UX designers to build the navigation system and overall user experience.

The Eight Principles of Information Architecture

IA's main point of attention is the user's goals. Its primary focus is the structure itself before the way it is then represented on screen. It heavily relies on the User Research done by the research team to gain an understanding of how users want to relate to the content and what kind of functionalities are expected. And it leverages the set of content and functionalities that can be supported by the structure.

Quite a few technical skills are involved, but keeping an eye on these eight IA principles, introduced by the amazing Dan Brown from EightShapes, is usually a good way when approaching the subject for the first time.

- **The principle of objects**

Treat content as a living thing, with a lifecycle, behaviors, and an emotional connotation. When starting a project, try and identify all the different content types and put them down as a framework to use throughout the site. It will give you an array of different ways to classify, sort, expose, and connect content together, creating meaningful relationships to complementary items or features.

- **The principle of choices**

Create pages with a range of choices focused on a particular task. Users shouldn't be spending time browsing through lists to find what they need. When designing information hierarchies, it is better to spread things out in shorter lists of choices to avoid overwhelming your users, and instead of helping them to achieve what they aim to.

- **The principle of disclosure**

Do not flood the page with information. Show only enough to help users understand what kinds of information they'll find as they dig deeper. Think of content. In terms of layers, disclosing one at a time as they escort people to their desired outcome.

- **The principle of exemplars**

Show the way. Describe the contents of categories by displaying examples of the contents.

When you design navigation, try to fit a few examples of the contents living under a category name. Especially in more complex architectures, these links provide quick understanding (and access) to the most common features of that particular category and save your user a good amount of time and cognitive load.

- **The principle of front doors**

Homepages are just one access, but there are many other doors and windows to your house. Assume at least half of the visitors will come through some page other than the home page, most of the time, through some link shared on social media or ranked on search engines. Therefore, each destination page has to help users understand where they are and what else they can find on the site. Users may have already found what they were looking for, but that page has the responsibility to give visitors a taste of what else they can do while they're here, too.

- **The principle of multiple classifications**

 There's no such thing as the ideal customer. Users may have different backgrounds and approaches. Try to offer a range of different classification schemes to browse the content. People may use topics to navigate, but they may also use the content type or author's pages. A well-designed navigation mechanism incorporates multiple schemes that let users employ them independently but also combine them if they feel to. Just remember to not exceed and overwhelm users.

- **The principle of focused navigation**

Don't mix apples and oranges in your navigation scheme. Instead, establish a clear strategy for finding content by purposely entwining different navigation mechanisms. Top navigation, sub-menus, topic research, related content. Be vertical and horizontal.

- **The principle of growth**

 Are you just dropping your website there without ever going to update it? Unlikely. Therefore you should remember throughout the design process that the content you have today is only a small fraction of the content you will have tomorrow. Plan spaces and navigation to be easily expanded or shrank over time. Design for growth, not for stillness.

The Four Systems of Information Architecture

In order to build a strong information architecture, your design process should lie onto four fundamental components, or system typologies, brilliantly identified by the incredible Lou Rosenfeld and Peter Morville, two giants in the field.

- **Organization Systems**

 An organized system is a framework whose role is to divide information into groups or categories so that the user can easily anticipate where they can find different pieces of information. Information architects and UX designers can tap into three main types of organization.

- Sequential organization systems aim to create a path for users, guiding them through the content to help them achieve their goals. This kind of system is better suited for apps or websites that need different layers of interaction, such as e-commerce checkouts.

- Hierarchical organization systems' main goal is to present each content piece based on its level of importance. This kind of system helps users to distinguish what is the most relevant content on the page, thanks to visual and dispositional clues. It is best suited for posters, book pages, landing pages, and so on.

- Matrix organization systems are meant to deal with many complex architectures since they enable the user to choose their own path through the content. Users are provided with choices and have to make decisions on their own. Of course, this kind of flexibility should also be planned, as too many choices can be overwhelming and make you lose users.

Other minor organization systems include alphabetical and chronological schemes, as well as systems based on topic or audience type.

- **Labeling Systems**

Information architects use labels to convey a large amount of information in just one or a few words. Our brain is capable of associating a cloud of concept revolving around a single word. This ability is triggered to communicate more complex meaning in little space, uniting data effectively, and enhancing the overall navigation as a consequence.

- **Navigation Systems**

The way people move through the page is the core interest of Information Architecture. When it comes to design the backbone of navigation, information architects deploy many techniques and tools to orientate the user through the content. The overall goal is to help them interact with the product successfully according to the desired outcome.

- **Searching Systems**

These systems are widely used by information architects on more complex and articulate websites with loads of information. They allow users to search for a specific keyword or information inside the product. An effective searching system allows users to apply filters to the research and provide a result page that helps them navigate through related informations too.

Where to Begin

Information Architecture is a broad field, and there are many other interesting aspects to cover, and it may be difficult for beginners to orient themselves through complexity. What I suggest is to lay the foundations of your knowledge regarding Information Architecture, starting from two key approaches: library science and cognitive psychology.

Library science goes as far as ancient Egypt with the Pinakes of the Library of Alexandria being the first book catalog ever recorded. Over the century, this science has evolved studying different effective ways to categorize and catalog information resources going from books to magazines. As a UX designer, you want to expand your knowledge with elements from library science to form a solid approach to define similarities and create metadata to assign to content.

Cognitive psychology studies how the human mind works and how it processes data. As we will cover later in the Visual Design Principles chapter, most of the design rules we use today are rooted in psychology studies. This is extremely valuable for Information Architecture as you need to know how to make the most out of people's mental models to orientate their eyes through the design. Visual hierarchy and Gestalt principles are a core asset for every designer, as well as some basic knowledge of how recognition patterns and cognitive load work.

User Journey

User journey is a visualization of the relationship existing between a user and a particular product or brand. User journey maps out the different touchpoints across the different channels, representing them on a timeline.

It is a crucial tool for UX designers because it allows them to see the interactions from a user's perspective, encouraging a more human-centered approach. It is a cornerstone for both the user experience team and the executives that want to track Key Performance Indicators of the product, thus becoming a cornerstone for strategic decisions in the design phase and in the iteration phase.

User journey is a flexible tool that can be used to represent the complete end-to-end experience with the brand or the product, or it can be narrowed down to focus on one particular interaction like checkouts or form filling. Having done your research properly is helpful here as the user journey should map the experience of one user persona. If there are multiple personas targeted, which is quite often the case, you should make different user journey maps for each to understand. How and where the experience will differ. Disposing of solid information about your user is essential here to avoid making false assumptions. Different users may have different expectations and approaches or come from different front doors at different times of the day. Be sure to describe a scenario for your persona to evolve into, and remember to make it as real as possible, with interferences and real-life context. People have specific motivations to interact with the product. Even urgent needs that they need to address while doing some other business. Different segments will have different reasons to accomplish a specific task. Creating a list of touchpoints (and pain. points) will help you manage this part, which can be tricky at first. Touchpoints are specific user interactions (and actions) that a user has with the product or brand.

Multiple channels mean multiple touchpoints, so be sure to include every relevant possibility.

All this information about the journey should be put together and sketched on paper or digitally, as a step-by-step interaction. Each step represents a chunk of the whole experience, which is an actual experience too. The experience can be positive at one touchpoint and negative at another, these ups and downs influence the way the overall interaction is perceived, leading to positive or negative emotions.

The resulting narrative should then be truthful, reflecting the actual user journey from their point of view, and not an idealized story built to confirm your design ideas. Try to validate it as soon as possible through testing sessions, or at least by revisiting User Research findings.

User Flows

User flows are visual representations of the many different paths a user can take when interacting with a product. It is usually intended for digital products, but I find it equally beneficial for physical products or broader experiences with a brand as a whole.

User flows can be drawn down on paper or made digitally with dedicated software apps. The outcome is called a flowchart. It starts from the very entry point, which could be a homepage or an article on the blog on digital products, or, if we're dealing with a physical product or service, the moment the user enters a shop or when it first push the power on button of a remote controller. The flowchart then goes through each touchpoint until the end of the experience. It can be a device turning off, checkout or payment, or even the confirmation email after purchase.

The different events of the flow are called nodes and are represented with various shapes indicating a particular type of process. Rectangles depict necessary tasks, while diamonds represent yes/no choices submitted to the user. Every node is also connected by lines and arrows, traced to visualize the different paths inside the product or service.

UX designers can choose among different types of flowcharts, depending on what they are creating. There is not a preferred solution here, so be sure to choose the flowchart type that better suits your needs for the particular product you are designing the experience for.

Let's take a moment to introduce a few of the most used typologies.

Task flows are the best choice if you are designing a low choice interaction that doesn't include multiple branches but one, or at most, very few pathways. Online forms are a perfect example of this kind of product. All users are meant to accomplish the same tasks in the same way, the path is rigid with no variability allowed.

Wireflows stand at the crossroads of wireframes and flowcharts. The diagram uses the actual layouts instead of the usually shaped nodes. They leverage the ability of wireframes to communicate the visual experience and can be beneficial to have a more complete vision. The downside is that they can add complexity to the diagram, making designers lose focus on the essential information a node is meant to convey. Wireflows are commonly used to represent mobile apps user flows, as the screen size remains manageable.

Traditional user flows to focus on the different pathways that might be taken by the target audience and the different target personas. They take into account the many differences among the users and represent different entry points and how these entry points direct the interaction of the specific user. While the main task to be accomplished is usually the same, user flows must display many different scenarios.

Whatever the type, flowcharts are extremely beneficial to the design process as they allow designers to evaluate and optimize the experience to meet both the business and the user goals. A flowchart can reveal futile steps that slow down the acquisition or conversion rate. Having them mapped out on a diagram is the best way to erase what is detrimental to the experience and add what might be missing. Therefore enhancing the clarity of the navigation through the product. All the many routes available to users should be optimized without exceptions. Again, we are talking about different persons interacting with the product, there is no preferred path, but rather only different paths that all have the same degree of dignity.

Flowcharts are also beneficial when it comes to redesigns. Mapping out the different patterns of interaction is the fastest way to identify pain-points and work out how to make the experience more smooth and efficient. A positive side benefit is that such diagrams are easily understandable by clients because they resemble project management and marketing charts and go straight to the point, eliminating the visual design aspect, which is the most commonly distracting feature of the product when dealing with executives.

Prototyping

A prototype is a rough version of a product that UX designers create during the design process. The ultimate goal of a prototype is to give a pre-definitive unified shape to the findings collected until this point. Building a prototype enables UX designers to test the flow of the product and the validity of their analysis and design ideas. Prototypes are then used to gather feedback on the product or service from internal parties, showing to stakeholders how the final product would look and function, but first and foremost, from the target audience. Thus, they are usually the endpoint of the design stage and the starting point of the testing stage.

Prototypes are fluid by definition, as they are meant to be tested and revised along the process, based on user feedback.

Basically, that's putting out the "product" to the world for the first time, and see if everything goes as planned. Spoiler alert: it usually doesn't.

To put it as David Kelley from IDEO,

> "If a picture is worth 1,000 words, a prototype is worth 1,000 meetings."
>
> - David Kelley

There are many types of prototypes a UX Design team can choose among. The choice depends on the stage you're at in the design process, the goals you have, and the available resources.

The discriminant here is the level of fidelity to the actual final product.

Low-fidelity prototypes are more than enough if you are willing to use them to present a semi-definitive version of your work to clients. High-fidelity prototypes, on the other hand, are preferred if the goal is to gather quality feedback from the target user and if you have already validated a series of design ideas in earlier stages.

Let's take a look at the different types of prototypes based on this definition.

Low-Fidelity Prototypes

Low-fidelity prototypes include:

- Sketched prototypes
- Paper prototypes
- Click-through prototypes

Their goal is to outline a product's flow and test its usability and functioning. They are the quickest and cheaper way to evolve your finding and design ideas into a tangible representation of the product. Even if they are not as aesthetically pleasing as high-fidelity prototypes.

- **Sketched Prototypes**

Sketched prototypes are the most rudimentary form of prototyping. They are usually pen-and-pencil drawings meant to map out the initial idea, and spark discussion among your design team or to confront with the development team.

The most straight-forward benefit is that it's fast. Sketches can be drawn in just one minute and the low-value we often attribute to this kind of process, helps the mind to roam free, boosting creativity. It also doesn't require coding knowledge, from you or anyone else, making it the best way to run collaborative sessions and include different points of view.

- **Paper Prototypes**

Paper prototypes are more defined than sketched ones. They are not freehand as sketches are, but rather involve the use of cardboards, stencils and other paper adds-on. They can represent screens of an app, but also a physical product with creative use of the origami and paper-fold techniques.

Like sketches, they are usually created at early stages because they are fast, easy, and inexpensive. Paper prototypes are extremely beneficial to UX teams to give a stronger sense of interacting with an actual product, requiring less imagination and allowing designers and developers to focus on more technical features.

- **Click-Through Prototypes**

Click-through prototypes are the most advanced type of low-fidelity prototypes. They use basic hyperlinks to get the user from one screen to the other, mimicking the experience and flow of the user. They are a little more time-consuming to make but are able to take things a step further, providing a stronger sense of what the final experience would look like.

They can be created from scratch with specific software apps, or just by using simple slide-making apps with simple links to the next slide. You can even upload your sketches from the sketched prototype if you want to save time.

High-Fidelity Prototypes

High-fidelity prototypes include:

- Interactive prototypes
- Digital prototypes
- Coded prototypes

Their goal is to get even closer to the actual final product. They are more advanced than their low-fidelity counterparts, bringing basic, or even advanced, functionalities to life. They are aesthetically pleasing and usually come later in the process when the UX Design team has a firm grasp of the overall product look and functioning. Thus, they are the best fit possible to conduct usability testing and refine the product before launch.

- **Interactive Prototypes**

Interactive prototypes stand a step further than click-through prototypes. They do not just make use of hyperlinks taking the user from a page-state to the other but provide basic interactivity. That means, for example, clicking a dropdown and seeing the menu appear on the same slide. Interactive prototypes provide a more definitive-look and useful feedback-response to user actions.

They are more realistic than any low-fidelity prototype, therefore better suited for gathering feedback. Especially for digital products, they can be made quite easily with specific software apps that already provide the most common components. Therefore, they commonly don't require coding skills or a huge budget and offer easy-to-understand drag-and-drop features. In my experience, I found out that interactive prototypes are. Best to produce before the product is under development. This way, there is still time to make changes.

- **Digital Prototypes**

Digital prototypes are the most common type of high-fidelity prototypes. They can be seen as interactive prototypes on steroids. They allow UX designers to create rich, interactive, and animated product prototypes that look very similar to the finished product, even with smooth transitions between pages. The most successful digital prototypes can even be real products, ready for implementation.

If you need to conduct accurate testing, digital prototypes are the best option. The user-interface is so realistic that many can't see the difference with the actual product. As you can imagine, they are a little more costly to resort to and maybe produced explicitly for final testing.

- **Coded, HTML/CSS Prototypes**

Coded prototypes are the most complex kind, the closest to the final product. They are, of course, the best fit to gather user feedback through testing. They look, and behave, just like the finished product, and can be hosted on any server, which makes them easy to share and test even at long distances, and across multiple devices. They provide all the transitions, interactions, and can manage dynamic data just like a regular product.

So why doesn't anyone go for coded prototypes? Well, they need time, money, and advanced programming skills to produce. Plus, they are not easy to revise once the necessity of making changes emerges. Therefore, before going for a coded prototype, you may want to have a strong level of certainty about your design choices.

4. Test and Measure

First off, a disclaimer. Most people blame UX Design, accusing it of killing creativity and resulting in outcomes that always seem to resemble each other. Is it true? Yes, but no.

Now that you've got your research done, and your prototype ready, it's time to test and gather feedback on the actual product. Why? Well, because the user knows it best. Simply. Your end goal as a UX designer is to make people's life easy, but you can't pretend to know if you succeeded in doing it if you don't test the product directly with them.

Let's cover some of the most popular techniques to do the testing, though.

Usability testing

Usability testing is the act of intentionally studying target users as they interact with a product prototype before fully developing it. The end goal of usability testing is to gather feedback to confirm or discard design choices made to this point. As a UX designer, you want to make sure that the purpose of the product, as well as the features and functions provided, are actually in line with what real people need. To achieve this knowledge, usability testing is absolutely key, as it allows you to observe how real-life people use your product.

Usability testing can be conducted in two different ways: lab usability testing and remote usability testing.

Lab Usability Testing

Lab usability testing is held in special environments, aka laboratories, and is supervised by one or more moderators. A moderated session is aimed to obtain real-time feedback on live users' actions while interacting with the product. A professional moderator should, in either case, remain discrete, asking questions only when it is necessary, and giving as little directions as possible to avoid ruining the authenticity of the interaction between the user and the product.

Moderated lab usability testing is the go-to method when you are looking for in-depth information on how real users relate to the product. The greatest benefit of this technique is that it allows UXers to investigate the reasoning and motivations behind user behavior. This way, you can get qualitative data that is crucial to orientate design decisions before full development.

By the way, lab usability testing is costly. You need to hire a trained moderator, provide a controlled environment with recording equipment, and, of course, you have to pay test participants. And you want to make sure that your user research has been well conducted.

Otherwise, you'll end up testing users that are not reflective of your real user base.

Remote Usability Testing

Remote usability testing occurs without a moderator. It is quicker and cheaper than lab usability testing for obvious reasons. Another interesting benefit is that, unlike testing in a controlled environment, participants are using the product in their own environment, with their own devices, and possibly when they might actually need to use your product. This leads to more natural behavior, but, on the other hand, not being able to ask questions or observe the body language, means that this type of testing collects less detailed results. Remote testing doesn't go deep into the reasoning and motivations behind a particular behavior, it just records actions, going for quantity over quality. Therefore it is better to have it well-planned with precise hypotheses that you want to validate.

Remote testing is achieved by recording sessions on apps or websites and allows UX designers to test large segments of users. Session recordings are rather simple to conduct. They involve installing software on a device or a plug-in into a website or app that records the actions that real users take when they interact with the product. Some even provide output under the form of a click-heat map.

It helps you understand what content or features users are most interested in, and what are the major issues they face while interacting with the product. As this method gathers quantitative data, it is always better to pair it with at least another technique to collect qualitative data as well. Pinpointing the problem is good, but you still need to understand why it is actually a problem for the user.

Guerrilla Testing

There's another not-much-talked-about way to conduct usability testing. It's called guerrilla testing. It is a hybrid method, particularly useful in the early stages of the design process, when you have a tangible low-fidelity prototype and want to know whether you're moving in the right direction or not.

    Guerrilla testing is the simplest and cheapest method of usability testing, which is great in the early stages. Practically, it involves going into a public space that might be relevant for your target audience (a coffee shop, waiting room, university campus) and ask people to interact with your prototype. In exchange, participants often get a small gift for their time, such as free coffee, but you can really get creative here.

    Therefore, guerrilla testing is a useful way of collecting personal opinions and emotional impressions about your design ideas and concepts, so you might want to consider to include it in your test plan. Just keep in mind that participants, while providing real user feedback, might not match your target users, as you are testing random people that will give you from five to fifteen minutes of their time.

Whatever the method you choose, always be sure to prepare a test plan before doing the testing. Determine the nature of your study, define what you are looking for, and why. Pinpoint specific areas or issues you want to focus on, and the type of users you want to test. Take the time to plan every session and every question, and don't forget to have the logistics figured out, too. Who is going to moderate the session, where are you going to conduct the test, how much time do you need the test to last, how much money can you spend?

Another overlooked aspect of usability testing is the pre-testing and post-testing data. Always remember to collect demographic and psychographic information before the actual test. Ask questions about how often the user has been doing a certain activity, when was the last time the user has done a particular task, what usually influences the user's opinion, etc. Also, reserve some time at the end of the usability testing session to ask follow-up questions, and gather final feedback from the participant.

A/B test

A/B testing, or split testing, is a method used by UX designers and marketers to compare two versions of something. Be it a product, an app, or an ad. The goal is to determine which one of the two versions is more successful, according to our business, product, and user needs.

Two versions of the product, A and B, are created and submitted randomly but in equal numbers to users. The version that measures the most users taking the desired action is the winner. This obviously implies that each user's response is recorded with some testing tool or analytics.

A/B testing comes handy when it comes to confirming a design is going in the right direction, optimize conversion rates, improve the overall user experience, decide which approach or tone to implement. Basically, A/B testing is where fortune-teller magic stops, and certitude takes the lead. No more, "I think this will work," you will be able to base your design decisions on solid, specific data.

When conducting an A/B testing campaign, you always want to have your goal clearly identified. Ask yourself what do you need to know in order to proceed with product development. Focus on one problem at a time, to be sure the collected data is clean. Form a clear hypothesis on which of the two versions your predict will work better, and explain why you expect this impact. Again be sure to avoid multi-variant testing, as increasing the test complexity means also taking the risk to deal with more messy and uncertain data.

Your testing plan should also have figured out how many responses do you need to get statistically relevant results. Many beginners make fall into the confirmation bias, and are not looking for actual answers, but rather want to confirm their predictions. Thus, be sure to have a clear table to make sure things are running correctly and stick to it.

Once you have the data gathered, implement the results, and go for incremental improvement, conducting new testings to go further and gain even more knowledge. The more you test, the more you know.

Biometrics

Technology evolves and gives us more and more tools to conduct in-depth testing. When talking about biometrics, we are talking about the future of UX research. While some of these technologies have been existing for a while, they are becoming cheaper and cheaper and thus more accessible for UX Design teams.

Let's dive into some of the most useful technologies to uncover users true emotions:

- Eye Tracking is a technology that tracks participants' eye movement. It enables UX designers and researchers to know what users are looking at, what path do their eyes follow, how long they're lingering on a specific element. The output looks just like a click-heat map but for the eye.
- EEG (electroencephalography) is a technology that measures electrical activity in the brain of a participant. As it uses electrodes connected to the head of the user, this technology enables UX

designers to learn about the emotions arising during the use of the product and to track cognitive activity and loads.

- GSR (Galvanic Skin Response) is a technology that measures the electrical conductivity into the small amounts of sweat generated by the pores on your skin. Like EEG, it is an advanced technology that can provide critical information about users' emotional states.

- FER (Facial Expression Recognition) is a technology that processes the variation in human face morphology when emotional states emerge. Modern artificial intelligence software is more and more accurate and provides a deep understanding of satisfaction and difficulty states that a user can encounter when using a product.

New biometric devices are increasingly practical and suitable for UXers. The possibilities are fascinating and little-explored yet. They are powerful tools for UX researchers and designers that can provide insights unachievable by other research methods.

The greatest benefit of this kind of approach is the ability to give insights about what attracts and engages attention. What sustains attention, and what emotional state is linked to a specific activity over a specific task. Understanding emotional engagement is key to craft a powerful user experience for the people.

These new technologies allow UX designers to gather data and make design choices based on what actually drives engagement and positive emotional-states, helping us build exciting experiences from start to finish.

We are entering a world of endless possibilities of which we have just barely scratched the surface.

Data and analytics

Analytics are everywhere. After conducting User Research and usability testing, UX teams are usually drowning in data. And that is good. I mean, really good. But a large amount of data is useless if you don't know what to do with it.

Many beginners get stuck here, so it is crucial to address the number one problem I've seen people do through the years.

There is no such thing as uninteresting data, but you have to be clear with your goal to extract meaning from them. Otherwise, you'll end up distracted, and you will fail to draw out actionable insights.

Do not focus on the tool, focus on the Why. If you rely on analytics tools to provide you the meaning you need, you will end up with nothing. Only you and your UX team know what do you actually need. Allow yourself to spend time thinking about the problem you need to address, and the result you are looking for. Why are they relevant? What actions will they foster when you find out the results?

When you have your objectives clearly drawn out, it's time to make a measurement plan.

- Define macro and micro, compulsory, and desired actions. Focus on each of these actions you want to analyze and look for potential issues in the user flows and journeys. Functionality is key, but you may want to measure the emotional response, too.

- Make hypotheses and try to prove them right or wrong, based on your overall objectives. The investigation may be about traffic, technical features, content, navigation, visual design. There is so much involved in the UX process. Just be sure to measure what is relevant for the product development, and what can affect the overall experience with the product or the brand.

- Triangulate. Use your qualitative findings from other research methods to drive your analysis. Use big data and analytics to prove or disprove these findings, collected with smallest parties, like it is often the case with usability testing.

- Expand your view. Never forget that there is much more than your product out there in real life. If users are not responding as you expect, where are they going instead to meet their needs?

Quantitative data and analytics are increasingly becoming a milestone in UX Design. As UX designers, we are called to learn and leverage this asset to gather important information and turning it into actionable findings. The biggest challenge is to get familiar with analytics systems meant for marketing purposes rather than UX purposes, therefore as UX professionals, our role is to determine where metrics can add value in those processes and where it is better to discard them and go for qualitative data instead.

Reports

Reporting is way too often overlooked when talking about UX. If you want your findings to be of any use, you must present them in a readable report. Just include pertinent information and just enough detail. Make the sections short, use tables, and visual examples such as screenshots and diagrams. Remember that the report should be designed to easily translate into concrete actions and design decisions.

So, what are the essential information to include in your report?

- **A Background Summary.** Describe what you tested, where you tested it, when the testing was conducted, and every relevant about the logistics. Most of all, focus on the why. What were you trying to achieve and why it was relevant to the design process. Include information about the testing team, the different hypotheses, and a brief description of the problems that you and your team encountered during the testing sessions.

- **Methodology.** As you include the test, a methodology is key to understand the validity of the result and to replicate the experiments in the future, which saves time and money. What have you tested? What metrics have you been monitoring? How have the participants been selected? Include information about them, and provide a brief summary of the demographic and psychographic data.

- **Findings.** This is the core of the report. Describe the results for each scenario and for each cluster of users. Indicate success and failure rates, as long as averages. The kind of data here really depends on what you've been testing and why. After providing both quantitative and qualitative data and metrics, give your interpretation as a designer and how the results will affect the design and development process. Each statement should be rooted in consistent data that you should present in a visual form, if possible. List your major findings and minor finding separately. Do not solely focus on issues encountered but also mention positive findings, as they validate your design ideas, and add to the credibility of your research activity. Sometimes users' comments can be illustrative, so you may want to include them, too.

- **Recommendations.** For a test to have any value, you must identify what you've learned and what you can do to improve the product according to the findings. Most of the time, you will not be able to implement all the recommendations. In those cases, including a priority list might be a good idea, so you can focus on addressing the most serious problems. Remember: the users' need comes first. Always.

5. Launch and Iterate

Final thoughts. You've done the research, you've developed a prototype, you've tested and corrected it, and then, finally, you've launched the product to the market. Good job, you surely deserve a little rest, but UX Design does not end just because the product has been launched.

The launch is not the end. It is only the beginning. When a product goes out into the market is precisely where you want to monitor how it performs. For the first time, you can have access to large-scale real-life data, mostly quantitative, but if the customer service is well defined and integrated, you may have access to qualitative data, too. Furthermost, you can target actual users that are actually using your product in their everyday life if you feel you need to do some further testing.

User experience really begins when everything gets real. Thus, as UX designers, our job is to keep our eyes open and iterate the UX Design process over and over again to perfection our product over time. It is an ever-going process.

I want you to remember that UX is about making people's lives easier. Think of your user, think of the issuers they're facing, think of what else can help them fulfill their needs, and make it happen.

Visual Design Principles

"Great designers understand the powerful role that psychology plays in visual perception. What happens when someone's eye meets your design creations? How does their mind react to the message your piece is sharing?"

— Laura Busche, Brand Content Strategist at Autodesk

Psychology is the key to design user experiences. Both when it comes to behavior prediction, and when it comes to using visual elements to help the user navigate through our design.

This is why visual perception is so important, and a good UI designer is often found among the UX Design team. In the following chapter, we will cover the fundamentals of visual design, starting from Gestalt basics.

Gestalt Basics

The Gestalt Principles are a set of psychology laws identified by German psychologists Max Wertheimer, Kurt Koffka, and Wolfgang Kohler in the 1920s. They describe how humans see objects by seeking patterns, similar grouping elements, and simplifying images. It is important to note that nothing physical is involved, this is not about the built-in receptors in our eyes, rather about how the information is processed by the human brain. This way, we can state that Gestalt Principles are in mind, not the eye.

The three psychologists demonstrated that human beings typically extract meaning from chaotic stimuli as a way to make sense of the world around them. A sort of natural compulsion to find order where there isn't, thus seeing sensible images that don't actually exist in the physical world but only in their mind. In other words, illusion.

> "The whole is other than the sum of the parts"
>
> — Kurt Koffka

Designers soon began tapping into these findings, leveraging their potential to engage users with brand logos and advertising. Over time they have developed tricks and best practices to make the most out of our natural tendency to seek order in pictures, refusing to process ill-ordered elements as they are.

The Gestalt Principles are decisive in UX design, in interfaces particularly, as users must be able to intuitively understand the design and quickly grasp how they can use it to reach their goals. UX and UI designers, have to appreciate the importance of Gestalt using this knowledge in order to guide users through the interface without confusing or delaying them, but rather helping them to find a way through their options and identify with the brand or product. Further, as the ones responsible for the human-centered design approach, designers must remember that even if these principles are universal to the human experience, they still have to be perfected and adjust to the cultural background and physical proficiency of the end-user.

But what are those principles in the first place? Let's dive into the seven most important ones:

- Figure-ground
- Similarity
- Proximity
- Common region
- Continuity
- Closure
- Focal point

- **Figure-Ground Principle**

The figure-ground principle illustrates how people perceive objects as either being in the background or the foreground. The elements of an image either stand out in the front (figure) or withdraw into the back (ground). Human beings dislike uncertainty, that's why they look for visual stability and coherence. Designers should avoid ambiguity at all costs, so the eye can catch the foreground first. This way, the user always knows what he should be focusing on and what he can safely ignore the layout.

In this ambiguous figure, depending on where one focuses his attention, there are either two faces looking at each other (in white) or an elaborate vase (in black).

- **Similarity Principle**

The similarity principle states that we tend to mentally group items when things appear to be similar to each other. This perceptive vision can be achieved using various design elements such as color, shapes, or organization. The human brain seeks similarities and differences and is naturally driven to link similar elements. Factors like symmetry and regularity also add to the mix by giving regular visual handles to identify patterns.

In the image below, there are five columns, each made of four evenly spaced squares. Three columns have light grey squares, one has black squares, and another one has white squares. Even to give a description of the image, I am forced to mentally divide the image into three distinct groups based on their color.

- **Proximity Principle**

The proximity principle shows how elements that are arranged close together appear more related than elements that are farther apart. It is one of the most powerful principles because it completely overrides other principles like the previous similarity principle. Our brain tends to mentally encapsulate together close objects, differentiating them from those that are separated by greater distances.

In the image below, we clearly distinguish two groups. One is made of two columns, the left one being darker and made of squares, the right one being lighter an made of circles, while the second group has only one column and is also made of dark squares.

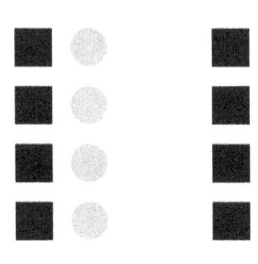

- **Common Region Principle**

The common region principle describes how elements that are visually enclosed in the same region tend to be perceived as a unique group. It is closely related to the proximity principle but can include much-distanced elements as long that they are bound together in the same closed region, delimited by a specific background tone or a border. This creates a perceived separation between the group and other separated objects, even if those objects are closer to some of the objects inside the region.

In the image below, you can see an array of dark dots evenly spaced. The dots on the left are separated from the rest by using a different color background that groups them into a distinct section.

- **Continuity Principle**

The continuity principle states that we perceive elements arranged in a line or curve as more related to each other, and our eye tends to follow them naturally, as continuation is a stronger signal than other similarities. We find meaning in it.

In the image below, our eye follows the curved dotted line even if the dots change color when they intersect the straight horizontal dotted line.

- **Closure Principle**

The closure principle illustrates our tendency to complete shapes, automatically filling in gaps between elements to perceive a whole image. When looking at complex arrangements, we search for a recognizable pattern to make sense of the chaos. If some shape has missing parts in it, our brain fills in the blanks.

In the image below, called the Kanizsa triangle, we perceive overlapping triangles and circles that, in reality, doesn't exist. They are complex shapes with missing parts that we are completing mentally.

- **Focal Point Principle**

The focal point principle states that our attention is immediately captured by elements that stand out visually. This can be achieved using a colored element in a black and white composition, leveraging size, spacing, or shading.

In this image, the light square takes and holds our attention because it has a different shape, value, and seems to be closer to the viewer because it overlaps the other shapes and has a drop shadow pulling it forward.

Other principles are the significance (we perceive ambiguous images as simple ones), good shape (we cluster elements together to complete familiar shapes), synchrony (we group elements that appear at the same time), and common fate (we isolate and unify elements based on their direction and pulling force).

Visual Design Toolkit

Apart from the Gestalt Theory, there are a number of principles and expedients that have been developed across decades of graphic and product design evolution. Let's examine a few of these to complete your toolkit.

Visual Weight

Some elements feel and look "heavier" than others in composition. It's an intuitive feeling, heavier objects draw the users' attention much more easily. The visual weight principle triggers exactly this phenomenon, to orient users' attention towards the things that matter, and provide a path to guide the experience.

It is worth noting that the visual weight of an object is relative to the spaces and objects that surround them. Therefore it is all about fine-tuning size, color, and contrast.

Contrast is about the visual difference between light and dark items. The more the difference, the higher the contrast. The right amount of contrast helps the eye to distinguish meaningful information in a layout, but an excessive amount of contrast can give a sense of disconnection and ruin the overall consistency of the design.

Size is a concept that is too often taken for granted, but I think that the "make the logo bigger" epidemic suggests to dedicate at least a brief comment to it. Size gives importance to elements, and can also convey information about depth, especially if blur and shadows are dropped in the mix. To achieve good design, a good visual hierarchy is needed. More important items should be bigger than less important ones to make information more readable, and the user experiences smoother and more enjoyable.

Color is also commonly used to define the hierarchy and status of the elements in a layout, especially on digital interfaces. By taking advantage of its three properties, designers can convey additional information without adding extra elements to the composition. Hue defines the actual color on the spectrum, Saturation defines the color intensity from subtle to vibrant, and value refers to how dark or light the color is. Contrast in color is a powerful way to bring information, for example, a greyed-out button appears as non-clickable, whereas a colored button looks plainly active. Moreover, in a layout, as is for typography, which we will not cover here, the combination of different colors, also known as color palette, can provide emotional information about the brand and product.

Room to breathe

The more elaborate or complicated the layout, the more likely it will create confusion and end up with flawed user experience. The minimalist "less is more" approach is gaining momentum, and that is wonderful news for UXers. The minimalist philosophy claims that each and every element presented should be useful and deliberate. No cluttering, no bullshit. Just the absolute essentials.

With the correct use of negative space, that is the blanks between content, the few elements in the composition stand out, being more attractive to the eye (someone said "Gestalt"?) without making the overall design feel empty. The breathing room created helps users keep the focus, and go straight to the point without useless distracting features or items.

A minimalist approach usually provides a highly usable design both in the aesthetic and in the content. Navigation is straight forward, and users are usually very happy with clear communication without distraction. A clean and essential design highlights content and empowers call-to-action prompts, which are also extremely beneficial for businesses.

Using motion to convey meaning

Hey! It's 2020! Today, motion is an essential part of the visual culture, and it should be in your toolkit as a UX designer. In fact, motion can describe spatial relationships between functionalities or states of the various elements. It can tell a story and lead the user through the composition, thus enhancing the user flow and creating a more natural experience.

Motion is one of my preferred personal ways to create better UX. Feedback is one of the areas where I find it more useful. Giving confirmation to the user helps to reassure that the product is functioning, and the actions taken are being processed. This can be especially useful when it comes to confirming password and emails in a form (think of the apple. Wrong password shake), or when a button is clicked.

Animations can also provide guidance on what the next steps are to reach the user's goal. They draw user's focus to specific areas, provide clarity and clues on what is about to happen. Rather than on a static interface, motion design can be leveraged to indicate the right elements at the right time. This makes the product more predictable and easier to navigate, filling potential comprehension gaps.

One extraordinary power that is way too often overlooked is the unique ability of motion to transform the visual hierarchy of an interface. Static pages aim for familiarity as a way to give certainties to the user, but this can become limiting as you may need a different spatial or content organization on specific pages that can be confusing. With motion, rearranging the visual organization is easy and even guides the user to the next view, opening new opportunities to a rich yet smooth experience. I think that in the UX realm, we've only been scratching the surface of the actual potential of motion, and I think designers should experiment and find new solutions to raise the bar and bring even better UX.

Last but not least, motion is the number one strategy to keep the user constantly engaged. It brings delight even in loading moments, or when dead ends are reached. Just think of the "no internet Dino" game of Google Chrome browser. It's so brilliant, there's even interaction in there!

Motion-based design can make a user experience memorable by making people feel they're interacting with something that is alive. It adds to the personality of the interface, as is to the conversation with the user, and helps strengthen the emotional connection with them. Simple attention to detail is often what signals to the people that there's someone behind the app that is thinking about them.

Thoughtful transitions and animations are a must-have in modern designs and should be taken into account during the UX workflow to craft an even better user journey, and enhance the user's experience. It can be both useful and delightful, but be careful: too much motion can be distracting, and we still want to help users easily solve their problems, so don't overdo it.

    Understanding how the human mind works make it easier to direct people's attention where we want to. UX designers should consider these principles all along the design process so that the product can accompany the user leveraging natural and intuitive behavioral patterns.

Going Further

Human Behavior and Motivations

Now that we've examined the design process and some visual design principles to guide you through your project, it's time to take a look beyond our backyard and go further into UX design.

As UX designers, our job is not limited to make things or applying some theoretical principles. Our job is to understand and interpret. We have to grasp human behavior and the motivations behind it. If we truly want our products to be successful and useful, helping tools in the hand of real people, then we have to dig in social sciences.

> "A designer who doesn't understand human psychologies is going to be no

more successful than an architect who doesn't understand physics"

- Joe Leech

Cognitive psychology, social psychology, neurosciences. Everything that shapes human behavior should be examined in depth. Understanding how social and family background influence our actions or how people's decisions and interactions can be influenced and manipulated is key to good design. Of course, ethics, too, plays a prominent role when it comes to influencing people's actions and thoughts. Design, like everything else, can be used for the bad as much as for good.

Anyway, we are not here to teach a class of philosophy nor psychology. What we'll do here is have a quick overview of the behavioral-psychology principles that are most important for UX designers. Ready?

- **The Kuleshov Effect.** It occurs when a user unconsciously makes up logical connections between two unrelated frames. This is what happens in almost every movie, but it is also what happens when the user ends up on a page or section he shouldn't have. Maybe by mistakenly clicking on a button, or because there was a flaw in the design. There are high possibilities that he will think there is an actual connection between his action and the result, and this can add to the confusion of your design.

- **Pavlovian Conditioning.** It is a learning procedure widely experimented and proven, which is most probably related to neuroplasticity. It is an associative learning process, repeated stimuli build memorized patterns in the brain so that we associate similar actions to the same reactions. For UXers Call to Action (CTA) buttons are a perfect example. Primary CTA buttons should have the same shape, color, and size, so it is easier for the user to get familiar with them and navigate through the design as they will expect the same result over and over again. Broken patterns are also used to trick users and make them click on buttons they otherwise wouldn't have even considered. This black method is extensively used on download websites that mimic buttons from familiar interfaces to get you to advertising pages or even to download malware onto your computer.

- **The Von Restorff Effect.** It is also known as the Isolation Effect. We've already talked about a similar effect in the gestalt theory of visual design. It states that an object that stands up from the rest is more likely to be remembered, as memory works in groups and categories. This is a fundamental psychological effect to tap on when designing the information architecture of a product. Shape, size, weight, color, even smell or sound can be triggered to orientate user action. Think about notifications. You look at your phone, and there is nothing wrong, but when you look again a few minutes later, a tiny green led immediately catches your attention, and you immediately know some notification has popped up.

- **The Chameleon Effect.** It is another well-known effect describing how people tend to unconsciously mirror other's behavior or emotional state when in close proximity. It is a way for humans to show they are paying attention to the interlocutor. It is one of the prominent ways we show empathy and trust. The reverse effect is also possible. Mentalists and persuasion experts have shown that deliberate mimicry of the other's gestures and words allows you to quickly trigger on empathy and establish a trusted relationship. Emotional design is a way designers are trying to tap into this effect to make interactions intimate and acquire customer loyalty.

- **The Paradox of choice.** This also is a powerful psychological effect every UX designer should know. Basically, it shows that the more choices we have, the less happy we'll be with our final choice. This is a piece of important information to remember when designing our product: this may seem counterintuitive, but too many paths and choices can end up in customer dissatisfaction. And we all want happy users, right?

- **The Aesthetic-Usability Effect.** Funny enough, this effect commonly occurs to designers! It makes aesthetically appealing designs look more legitimate and makes us think that pretty things are more intuitive than ugly ones. When reality knocks, however, we blame ourselves for not being able to understand this design that is clearly a high-end level. This is the most perilous trap for designers, that will then start to design for other designers and not for real people. Try to remember this next time you see a design on Dribbble that impresses you.

- **The Mere-Exposure Effect.** The term is self-explanatory enough, so I won't stay long on it. This effect explains how we are more likely to develop a preference for something or someone simply because we are familiar with them. The more we see it, the more we like it. For UX designers, it is vital to simulate this sensation of familiarity.

- **The Placebo effect.** It is a psychological effect that responds to the need of reassurance humans have. As human beings, we like to be told that everything's going good, or that everything will resolve well, or we like to think that we are in control. Either way, UX designers should always keep at the front of their mind that users need to be reassured, especially if they're using the product for the first time. Ever noticed the little "pull-to-refresh" animation on smartphones? That's exactly that.

- **The Serial-Position Effect.** It manifests when a list of things is presented to us. Studies have shown that we are most likely to remember the first and last items of the series, while we neglect the ones in the middle. This is why when building up your design, you should always place the most relevant information at the top or bottom of the list while relegating less meaningful information in the middle.

Create Trust

Trust is the number one key to successful business and product. Therefore, as UXers our job is to establish that trust with the user. Nowadays, most of the products out there ask users for something, is it some payment information or an email address, but asking a stranger is not that polite right? So to have a good experience, products should make every effort to help users understand why the information or task is needed. The provided reason should be meaningful and accompanied by honest and clear communication to increase the trust levels (and the conversion rates, don't forget we're also working for business here!).

Crafting a good user experience designers should remove doubt, making it easy for the user to understand what is needed and why. That way, the product, and overall experience end up being more enjoyable, and customer loyalty will increase dramatically.

Building trust is not an easy task in days like ours where the offer is huge, and people tend to be more suspicious. Here are some general guidelines to help you design your way through user trust.

- **Clear communication is key.** Honesty is a universally valued trait, and when you're asking for people's money, information, or even time, you can't pretend the user's trust if you're not presenting clear information.

- **Always protect your users.** People want to feel safe and worry about getting harmed in some ways. Emails, credit cards, sensitive information are personal, and users want them to be secured. As a designer, you have to avoid data breaches at any cost, and if a breach eventually happens, you should already have strategies to solve the issue quickly and show the user how much you care about their security. The same goes for any kind of product. Defective technology or potential risk with food should trigger an immediate recall strategy with refunds and new deliveries as soon as problems are solved. Make people feel protected, and they will trust you.

- **Consistency, consistency, consistency.** User experience is just like a conversation. You want to know who you're talking with, you want to identify the key characteristics of the person in front of you, tall, short, amusing, serious, gaudy shirts, casual outfits, what does he or she like. A brand strategy here is a fundamental asset for UX designers to work with. The product or service should have a clear identity, repeated consistently across every media, and supports. An unstable identity generates confusion and distrust, so don't overlook the importance of consistency.

- **Behind the scenes.** Show users there are humans just like them behind the product! Establishing a human connection is as important as transparency when it comes to building trust in the relationships between your product and users. Show how and why you work, show who's part of the team. Just add a human touch, and gaining trust would be easier.

- **Deliver useful content.** Would you still be talking to your friend if he didn't give you back? If he wasn't giving you affection, fun moments, deep conversation, or support? When crafting user experiences, designers should not limit themselves to design the actual interaction with the app or product, but each and every interaction with the brand. A content marketing strategy is a powerful tool to deliver meaningful content to the user.

This leads us to the last principle.

- **Keep up the conversation.** The more a user engages with your product or brand, the more familiar they will get to you, and the more trust they will place in you (do you remember the Mere-Exposure Effect?). Therefore, user experience should extend beyond the boundaries of the actual products and join the conversation with users where they like to spend their time: on social media, or at social events.

Of course, the golden rule still applies here: practice empathy throughout your process. If people feel they are just numbers to you, they will look elsewhere. I know that's easier said than done, but luckily we have a tool that's right here to help us out.

The Empathy Map

The Empathy Map helps UX designers develop a deeper understanding not only of the user but of the person they are designed for. It is a beloved tool of mine because it often reveals unexpected insights about persons and their needs! It allows us to synthesize and sum up the observations gathered during the research stage and draw more empathy in the design process.

The Empathy Map consists of four quadrants, each dedicated to investigating a different aspect of the person's reaction. It can be used to map out your observation during user testing or user research, but can also be very useful when constructing personas.

The four key traits are Said, Did, Thought, and Felt. What the user said when interacting with your product, what he actually did, what he thought, and what he intimately felt. Observing the first two aspects is usually easy, but determining the thoughts and emotions involved is a little bit trickier.

The number one solution is to ask the tested user to speak out their thought during the observation. This speeds up the process, but mind that not all thought is conscious, so you still have to work it out by interpreting gestures, and actions. Searching for subtle body language clues, tone of voice changes, or hesitations is the preferred means by which UX designers dig into the user's motivations, needs, goals, and feelings. What do they tell you about potential hidden emotions and desires? Note that needs have to be defined as verbs, not nouns. They are actions that lead you to define solutions.

Remember when I said great designers should have at least a basic psychology knowledge? Now you know.

Synthesizing all these observations in our Empathy Map helps UXers define their design challenges and pitfalls, and therefore craft better user experiences, perfectly suited for the target users.

Accessibility

And talking about empathy and design, are we talking about empathy for all? Or just about empathy for people like us?

> "When UX doesn't consider ALL users, shouldn't it be known as "SOME User Experience" or... SUX?"
>
> - Billy Gregory

Billy Gregory is a Senior Accessibility Engineer that shouted his thoughts on Twitter a while ago, raising awareness on a pretty serious and sadly common issue.

Most of the designs out there are made for what designers think are "standard" people (sigh), and completely overlook so many people with any sort of disabilities. Think of blind, deaf, or mute people. Think of colorblind people or persons who've lost or were born without some fingers, or even amputated people.

They are human beings too, why do they need won't deserve the same attention?

I think Billy Gregory struck a chord that needed to be struck.

Accessibility is a beautiful yet abused word. Manuals are full of it, and when you're just a student, you think, "yeah, of course, I will design for all." Then you start working for clients, and time and budget are limited, and you have to meet expectations and deadlines, so you start cutting out what you think you can sacrifice. Cynicism starts to surface, and you find yourself thinking, "how many people with disabilities are among my potential users? 5%, maybe less. Designing for the 95% will be fine."

I'm uncomfortable admitting it, but I've been there too, and frankly, it SUX (pun intended).

As UX designers, we are responsible for the user experience of all, not just user experience for some. Accessibility is a serious matter, and it has to be considered in every step of the design process if we really want to give the same opportunities to everyone without any discrimination.

How does your design work with users who need assistive technology? There is plenty of people who need screen readers or are limited to use a keyboard. Does your website or app have a mode for colorblind so they can navigate it? How is your pub counter accessible to a person on a wheelchair, or a small person?

This, of course, doesn't only apply to digital products, physical products, services, and spaces are also concerned. Bars and public spaces should be designed for people in wheelchairs too. Services like call centers should give users a choice between keyboard commands and voice commands. Otherwise, persons who are unable to use their fingers quickly will be left out. We've been talking about disability, but what about aging? By 2050 two billion people will be aged 60 years and older. Are our cities and products ready? Something as simple as the character size on a restaurant menu can be critical when losing eyesight. Are we really letting our parents and our future selves being a constraint to pull out their magnifying lenses each time they want to eat sushi?

As you can see, the case for accessibility is huge. If we truly want to build a better world, we have to think about everyone. Our design choices shape the world we live in. I think it's time to take some responsibility.

Customized Experiences

Customized experience is a fundamental part of what I call the "accessibility mindset." We're all different, and all worthy. When working on a project, UX designers should always think of all the differences among their supposed user base. This implies specific attention to people with disabilities, and more.

Maybe you are designing an e-learning platform to help underprivileged people get access to education. That's very noble, but have you thought for a second how they are going to reach your website? Maybe your users have low-speed internet or even no internet at all. They probably haven't got a shiny retina iMac on their desk, and will access your website using low-resolution screens. Having no computer but just some low tier smartphone is also a possibility. Always do your research, and always think of any implication. Empathy is key.

Technology is giving designers the ability to create custom experiences for everyone, in content, and in shape. Barriers can be tear down, if only we designers will be willing to spend more time and effort embracing human diversity.

From a content point of view, we're already doing that, with customized ads, suggestions, and everything related to big data and data analytics. The movies you'll see on the Netflix homepage will be different than mine and so on.

On the contrary, when it comes to the shape point of view, in other words, when it comes to user flows and information architecture, today most products, especially digital products like mobile apps, software, games, websites, are giving every user the exact same experience. The Netflix example perfectly fits here too.

There are some interesting exceptions, though, to which people are increasingly getting accustomed. Here are three basic examples of well designed customized experiences in the digital realm.

- **Character size.** Character size preferences can be found on almost every device nowadays. Kindle readers have it, smartphones and tablets have it, computers and web browsers too. But there is still plenty of room to expand this, and I'm thinking of software and mobile apps, and even ATMs or automated ticket kiosks.

- **Safari Web Reader.** If you are using Safari to browse the internet, you might have noticed a little paragraph icon on the top left of the URL bar. When you click or tap on it, the page layout transforms completely and allows you to choose the background color, and the character size and style, so you can read the page more comfortably. Many designers are pissed off because it ruins their beautifully and carefully crafted design, but hey, remember you are designing for the people, not for yourself or fellow designers. And you can still update your website, adding accessibility preferences. I'm sure people won't tap on that little Safari icon anymore. As we already discussed in the design process chapter, the design is an iterative process.

- **Dark mode.** Dark modes and Night modes are going increasingly popular, and I'm so happy! Using a backlighted screen device at night has been a pain for at least 20 years, even more, if you want to go back to the birth of personal computers. Now many apps, websites, and devices are giving users the opportunity to switch to more yellowish lighting that minimizes eye strain and reduces the blue light emitted by smartphones and tablets. Dark mode goes even further and allows people to invert the balance of black and white, darkening the background and reducing significantly the amount of light getting into your eyes from a close distance.

Allowing people to adjust the design to their needs is the next big step for UX Design, and it's taking off. I hope more and more designers will be concerned about this philosophy and approach the design of user experiences with a different eye: each and every human matter.

The Essential Value of UX Design

UX Design matters. We've already seen plenty of reasons why it does in this very book, but I want to break them down even further. Experiences are what people remember. No one recalls technical stuff with a smile on their face. UX Design is in a position to have a dramatic impact on how people see and feel the world around them. In fact, user experience is capable of shaping the world, directing efforts, and opening new possibilities to evolve as human beings. This is why I think it is important to have a clear understanding of the three macro benefits that UX Design brings to our society.

User Benefits

Our users are not just ours. They are users of many different devices, apps, spaces, services, and they come in an infinite variety of different combinations. They conduct busy lives, and they often have to deal with multiple problems across the day.

Good UX Design makes their lives easier, and can ultimately improve their quality of life. Just think about how a better performing computer can free up hours of our time. Time we are then able to dedicate to our passion or to our loved ones. That's what I'm talking about.

Whether they are essential, primary, or complementary, products play a significant role in the user's life. Products with a good user experience design reduce the cognitive overload of the user, they give them time and/or moments of joy because they are crafted upon their needs.

Well designed products help solve problems with which people are struggling in their everyday life. But great designed products can achieve even more. They can enable change, open doors, give access to areas that were formerly inaccessible. There is a great example that I want to share with you, it is called Liter of Light.

Liter of Light is a project that uses inexpensive, readily available materials to provide high-quality solar lighting to people with limited or no access to electricity. Giving access to lighting to over 300,000 households, Liter of Light has enabled thousands of kids to study at night, doing their homework and advancing in education. It has enabled thousands of people to learn new skills and build the product themselves. It has given hope, lighten up ideas, and opened up new exciting opportunities to many persons that otherwise wouldn't have had them.

Good UX benefit users in infinite ways, and to the extent that is largely overlooked. Whether you are providing lighting to people in poverty or giving free access to self-development books while waiting at the local post office, UX improves people's lives. And if that is not a benefit, I don't know what it is!

Product Benefits

You've got that idea of a new wonderful product you want to launch to market. Great! But I have to warn you, even if I don't know what your product is about yet, I can already tell you that it will probably fail.

According to Clayton Christensen, professor at Harvard Business School, there are over 30,000 new products introduced every year, and 95 percent fail. If you want to be in that 5 percent of successful products, it's either one or the other. Either you intensely pray to God for good luck, or you invest in UX Design.

User experience from early stages helps confirm that you are designing the right product, responding to the existing needs of real people. The whole user-centered UX process is the key to understand the who, the what, the how, the when, the where, and mostly the why. UX research provides information about the end-user of the product, when and how the user will use the product, and the main issues the product has to solve. It doesn't take a genius to understand that user research, prototyping, testing, and iterating are critical to product success. Allow me to paraphrase the legendary quote from Red Adair to stress out this concept:

"If you think it's expensive to go through the UX Design process, wait until your product fails to the test of the market!"

Or better put by Dr. Ralf Speth, CEO of Jaguar Land Rover:

> "If you think good design is expensive, you should look at the cost of bad design"
>
> - Dr. Ralf Speth

It is far less expensive to prevent an issue or usability problem from occurring in the first place than to fix it later with a costly redesign while already losing money on the market. UX Design saves time and money by creating the right product right from the start by gathering the information to build an ideal solution. And as it is often said, a problem well stated is a problem half solved.

According to a 2009 special report from Strategic Data Consulting, 80 percent of the unanticipated fixes during development are related to the user interface, and only 20 percent are due to actual bugs. This can be avoided through effective UX practices. And to further highlight the UX Design impact on a product ROI, let me bring you one last argument from Dr. Roger S. Pressman, an internationally recognized software engineer:

> "For every dollar spent to resolve a problem during product design, $10 would be spent on the same problem during development and $100 or more if the problem had to be solved after the product's release"
>
> - Dr. Roger S. Pressman

I think this definitely closes the case.

Business Benefits

Product benefits are already business benefits as the second president of IBM, Thomas J. Watson, clarified 50 years ago.

> "Good design is good business"
>
> - Thomas J. Watson

UX Design brings a lot of value to businesses. Incorporating design requirements upfront, doing the research and testing, and knowing the end-users the development process of products and strategies speed up dramatically, increase user satisfaction, and eliminate redesign costs.

One of the most overlooked business benefits is the increase in sales. A well-designed product provides a significant competitive advantage. Great user experience is a key brand differentiator for users that will likely overtake the price and allow the company to acquire more customers. Further, a useful, beautiful, and intuitive design encourages customer retention, with people wanting to keep using the product. Familiarity and trust can then even allow upsell strategies and increase the overall benefit for the business.

More money then. And less cost too. A well-designed product just works. Therefore fewer people will need support, and customer service costs dramatically shrink. A product that is poorly designed, because the user experience design was "too expensive" and had been skipped entirely, there will be an increased need for support, documentation, and training later on. Which translates into higher costs. Going through the UX Design process puts less stress on both employees and the bottom line in the long haul. Allowing the user to be less confused, more productive, and focuses will increase the amount of time spent on the product and strengthening the relationship between user and brand.

The financial impact of increased productivity is substantial and readily apparent on the company side too. Think of the development process. As they are responsible for the overall experience and as they always have to see the big picture, UX designers work closely with every actor involved in a product's development. Developers, UI designers, engineers, executives. This saves time upfront, and with the toolkit and skills of the UX designer, the company can conduct lean experiments, sprints, ongoing data analysis, market research, and optimization with ease. This avoids redoing things over and over again. An estimated 50 percent of development time is spent fixing mistakes that could have been avoided if the company had decided to go through the UX Design process. Incorrect assumptions on user behavior and lack of research and testing often lead to useless features and confusing designs that end up in countless headaches and even more loss of money. Instead, by carefully crafting the user experience, companies can decrease maintenance and development time and costs.

UX Design Jobs

What Does a UX Designer Do?

A UX designer's goal is to make people's life easier by providing beautiful solutions. UX designers are there to make technology, products, services, and spaces usable, accessible, and enjoyable for humans. They usually work as part of a larger team, responsible for bridging the gap between business stakeholders, end-users, and the development team. The UX designer is the one guy in charge to ensure the product actually smoothly solves the user's problem. A satisfying product is key to obtain customer retention and therefore meeting the business goals of the company.

UX designers work on a wide array of different projects: websites, mobile apps, software, augmented reality, virtual reality, internet of things, everyday-use objects, spaces, wayfinding systems, customer services, hotel stay, and on and on and on.

When it comes to everyday tasks, these will also vary depending on the project, the company or client you're working for, and many other variables. Generally speaking, the tasks involved are included in the process we outlined in the previous chapters and can involve elements of project management, business analysis, research, testing, psychology, designing flows, personas, wireframing, prototyping, and determining the information architecture. The only aspect in which the UX designers are usually not involved in the visual design of a product.

The disciplines of UX Design

As we already covered, UX Design offers plenty of flexibility in activities and job titles, but we wouldn't be UX designers if we haven't found some structure to describe our own field, right?

Here's where the Quadrant Model comes in. The four fundamental disciplines of user experience mapped out to explain the UX multidisciplinary realm, which involves elements of computer science, cognitive psychology, communication design, engineering, and much more.

Without further ado, I present to you the four building blocks of UX: Experience strategy, Interaction Design, User Research, and Information Architecture.

Experience Strategy (ExS)

Experience strategy is the quadrant involved in planning a holistic business strategy, incorporating the user's needs as well as those of the company. It is where business and design merge.

Interaction Design (IxD)

Interaction design is in charge when it comes to observing the actual interaction with the product. It considers every interactive element, such as animations, transitions, buttons, and other features. It is where device interface design and software design meet to create instinctive designs that enable users to smoothly complete every task up to their end goal.

User Research (UR)

User Research involves the identification of a problem to be solved. Extensive research and continuous feedback are required. The main tools used here are surveys, interviews, focus groups, usability tests, and everything that helps UX designers to gather data and turn it into good design decisions. It is where market research and design research blend.

Information Architecture (IA)

Information Architecture takes care of the organization part. Content and information have to be organized in an accessible and meaningful way to help the user navigate their way to their desired outcome.

Information Architects are mainly responsible for the relationships that run through the different elements of the product, the inner and hidden meaning of the user journey, and flow. Consistency throughout design, features, and language is carefully crafted to deliver a better possible experience. In other words, it is where design and library science meet.

Within these areas, you'll find a great variety of different job titles. UX Design is an ever-growing, fast-evolving field, offering countless opportunities to diversify and specialize. Let's list a few examples just to give a taste of the exciting possibilities of UX.

Voice designers work in the rising field of voice and speech recognition. They dedicate to create user-friendly interactions with voice technologies. Think of Alexa, Siri, Cortana. Someone has to design their tone and personality, someone has to write scripts and dialogues!

UX writers are the ones who handle the copywriting part of the job. Words are equally important as visual clues in the user journey. Remember that good UX has to be a pleasant conversation! It is also a good entry point for copywriters that want to switch their career.

UX developers are in high demand lately. That is because the glass wall that was keeping developers and designers separated is finally being thrown down. With the advances in technology, designers have to learn some coding skills, and developers have to learn some visual design skills.

These were only three of the countless potential ramifications of the broad UX field. UX Design is key to a product, and hence to business success, that is why UX jobs are on the rise. According to Glassdoor, UX Design was one of the 25 highest paying entry-level jobs of 2019, with an average of $80,000 earning per year for junior UX designers. The average salary of a UX designer then grows to almost $90,000. And companies are battling to hire the best. Will they be freelance, agencies, or employees.

Among the many reasons to become a UX designer, and past the mere salary argument, one could think of how big the smartphone and interactive devices have gone. How Artificial Intelligence and the Internet of Things are going to change the world and how exciting the idea of shaping the future is. Have you noticed how big fin-tech and health-tech are becoming nowadays? It is just the beginning. As UX designers, we could help save lives by designing smart products and fast, easy apps. We could help spread knowledge around the world or ensure transparency in this far west of data collection that threatens our privacy.

The opportunities are countless, and the moment is right. It's up to you!

Common Tools

Here is a list of the most common tools used by UX designers that help them to craft great user experiences.

It all begins with the identification of the who, the what and the why of your project. In other words: research. When gathering user insight, the key is to make it easy for the user to participate.

Tools for research and inspiration

- **Typeform** helps UX designers create forms, surveys, and quizzes. The free account includes up to 10 fields and 100 responses per month.

- **SurveyMonkey** is another popular tool for UXers when it comes to online surveys. There is also a useful feature called Audience that comes in handy when conducting large-scale-projects.

- **Skype/Zoom/Facetime** is the best choice for video interviews. A face-to-face chat is more than often necessary when gathering feedback.

- **Optimal Sort, Simple Card Sort, and Usabilitest** are useful tools that allow you to conduct remote card sorting sessions online.

When you're done with your research, it's time to get creative, experiment, and try to find the right solution.

Tools for sketching

You don't need any specific tools for sketching. Pencil and paper are more than enough to do the job. But then you may want to have your sketches organized all in one place.

- **Usability Hub** is a popular tool where you can upload your sketches and make preference tests.

Tools for Information Architecture

There is plenty of software that allows you to build an Information Architecture, but few are simple enough to make the experience enjoyable, and easy to manage (ironically, few have a good user experience).

- **Draw.io** is a completely free tool, both for personal and professional use. It automatically plugs into Google Drive, and has integrations with JIRA and Confluence, too. It is excellent for creating user flows, diagrams, flowcharting, and build information architecture. It also offers a free offline version.

- **Lucidchart** is similar to Draw.io with some additional features like pre-built templates and many more integrations. It also has a mobile app and support for business.

- **Omnigraffle** is a long-time excellent software in the IA industry. It provides AppleScript and JavaScript automation. It is a Mac-only software, though.

- **Visio** is another long-timer but has migrated to the online world, while the previous version stays Windows-only. It works excellently for IA design.

The next step is to turn your sketches and maps into actual wireframes and then transform everything you've done so far into a practical small-sized prototype that gets you closer to the final product!

Tools for wireframing and prototyping (digital products)

- **Invision App** is a powerful co-creating tool that can be seen as a digital whiteboard. It is useful to brainstorm, map, and even get feedback. It comes with many different features, like Freehand, Inspect, and DSM, that help UXers to quickly upload wireframes, choose a device, and start adding hotspots. It also helps to connect code and design with its Design System builder so teams can work faster, smarter, and more in sync.

- **Balsamiq** is one of the best low-fidelity wireframing tools in the industry. It gets rid of it. Every distraction and help you focus on structure and content.

- **Sketch** is a software that enables us to effortlessly create and prototype, keeping the whole team together and with a set of useful features to share with clients and easily move the design to development.

- **Mockplus** provides a handy drag-and-drop feature that can save tons of time.

- **Adobe XD** is a powerful, collaborative platform that helps you create designs for websites, mobile apps, voice interfaces, games, and more. Some of its features help you animate elements across the layout and reuse components.

- **Proto.io** allows users to create fully-interactive high-fidelity prototypes that look and work like a regular app should without needing a line of code.

- **Marvel App** is another useful tool for making interactive mockups, from wireframe to prototype, from low to high fidelity, from automated development to user testing.

- **Figma** is a cloud software that offers any feature you can imagine from the arc tool to sharing and co-creation functions. It allows UX designers to craft animated prototypes and test concepts.

- **Wireframe.cc** is an essential website that gets you immediately into the job without any distraction. Open and start wireframing. That's it.
- **Canva/Photoshop/Illustrator/Affinity** are other regular design tools not specifically made for UX Design, but that can come in handy if you are familiar with them.
- **Protoshare** is also a powerful tool to create realistic-looking digital prototypes.

Tools for testing

- **HotJar** is a useful tool to conduct session recordings.
- **VWO** is an incredible resource when it comes to conducting A/B testing campaigns.
- **iMotions** is a powerful tool for facial expression analysis and gaining deeper insights into users' emotions.
- **xLabs, ITU Gaze tracker, and Gaze Pointer** are three great tools to conduct eye-tracking testing.

Conclusion

Humans build systems to run societies in a never-ending attempt to make them more efficient and able to guarantee their inhabitants' well-being. Our well-being. Systems shape our lives and our understanding of the world. Crafting those systems is the office of UX designers. Think of the power and possibilities this implies.

> "With great power comes great responsibilities" - Uncle Ben, Spiderman

Everything is a system. As a UX designer, you have to think about the big picture. Mind the relations and flows, think of how things can be improved. From an app menu to the unintended queue that forms outside an ice cream shop. You have to focus on every part of the user journey, improving the local experience, the digital experience, and the emotional baggage the overall experience carries with it.

We are human beings, we are subject to many forces, internal and external. We are affected by the context of where we are evolving. Everything has to be taken into account. User satisfaction is not just user satisfaction. It is person satisfaction. You have the power to give people tiny moments of happiness or relief, reducing stress, and cognitive overload. As UX designers, we are eliminating obstacles. Imagine for a minute if every experience was carefully designed, how happier the whole world would be.

UX designers are donating freedom of mind and smiles to people. They are the invisible hand that guides us to achieve our goals. Experience is the only way through which human beings live life. I'm convinced that UX Design can have an impact on people's life, even if tiny. And I like to think that UX Design makes a difference in the world.

Teachers and nurses are some of the many careers that are focused on helping people. But there are other jobs that, while not being directly aimed at it, are nonetheless helping people indirectly. Most of the time, unnoticed. It is the case of User Experience designers.

In this book, we've seen how UX Design is a human-centered approach that relies heavily on empathy and psychology, ultimately focused on solving people's problems. By leveraging their skills and talents, UX designers can foster meaningful change and drive the world toward social good. Whether we acknowledge it or not, you and I can have a significant positive impact on the world. If you are looking for a career in which to feel fulfilled, and make a difference, then UX Design might be the best choice for you.

> "I always wondered why somebody doesn't do something about that. Then I realized I was somebody"
>
> - Lily Tomlin

You can help achieve the change you want to see in the world by shaping the future through design. As ultimately system builders, UX designers are like secret agents of change (always remember that good design is invisible to the eye). They dedicate to understand people, empathize with others, and give them the tools they need to fulfill their needs. In the end, we're making people's life easy. This approach allows UX designers to find problems with a high potential for social impact.

It is also a work that encourages humility and broad thinking. Always be reminded that "you are not the user", that you should "think of others", and "find solutions to people problems" helps UX designers become better persons. It is, by all means, a personality-shaping job.

In addition to that, the ability to address problems and quickly come up with wireframes and prototypes is a highway to creating socially impactful solutions. This could happen at work, with your team, or through a collaboration with a great client, but can also occur while applying your skills alone, in your spare time, to the causes you care for. Damn, I just hope there will be more and more UX designers out there in the years to come!

Carrying on personal projects with full control and responsibility can be challenging and quite rewarding when you achieve direct results for the people you care about. If I may, I would like to encourage you to think big. As UX designers, we already have the ability to collaborate with many other talented people with different personalities and skillsets. Reach out to them and scale up!

That's exactly what great Jason Ulaszek was thinking when he created UX for Good, a not-for-profit organization dedicated to leveraging the UX discipline to help solve pressing, complex social challenges. Because hey, what if the best designers in the world focused on its hardest problems?

As a designer and moreover, as a user experience designer, you have the opportunity to create significant social good. Just start a small, little project, small prototypes, become more and more ambitious, and then change the world with your peers!

I wanted to end this book with positive energy, and I hope you felt it through the pages. I really hope UX Design 2020 has helped you better understand what UX Design is, what process and skills are involved, and what UX designers actually do. I also hope this book has prompted you to look differently at the world of design. There is much more than stylish icons and beautiful color composition. This is really a field where you can get in contact with every kind of topic and profession, growing as a person and as a professional.

I hope this book, while being introductory, has given you the big picture, and that it has inspired you to take the step to join the UX community. It is a field with countless opportunities, even if most of our work remains invisible to the many. In fact, the less one notices our work, the best our design is. By the way, to quote The Secret Life of Walter Mitty,

> "Beautiful things don't ask for attention."

And to say it with the Little Prince,

> "What is essential is invisible to the eye."

Thank you.

Theo Farrington

Get in Touch

Let's spread positive design and use our UX-Superpowers to change the world together!

Get in touch to get free updates from the UX realm and get exclusive insights on my upcoming projects.

Opt-in at:
https://bit.ly/Theo-Farrington-UX

Thank you!

About the Author

Theo Farrington is a senior UX designer and director at an intentionally small and smart UX agency that helps worldwide businesses and tech startups to attract and retain customers by design. His secret? He combines product, business, and user goals to create value for all. But, shhh tell no one!

He has been to Rhode Island and studied design, kickstarting his career as a freelance graphic designer, but then found in User Experience Design a more meaningful way to use his skills. He firmly believes that the UX design approach is the key to a better world.

Made in the USA
Coppell, TX
04 December 2020

43031114R00154